THE FOOD AND COOKING OF
SCOTLAND

DISCOVER THE RICH CULINARY HERITAGE OF THIS HISTORIC LAND IN 70 CLASSIC STEP-BY-STEP RECIPES AND 300 GLORIOUS PHOTOGRAPHS

CLASSIC DISHES FROM HAGGIS TO DUNDEE BEEF STEW, AND FROM SCOTCH BROTH AND SALMON FISHCAKES TO WALNUT AND HONEY TART

CAROL WILSON AND CHRISTOPHER TROTTER

southwater

This edition is published by Southwater, an imprint of Anness Publishing Ltd, Hermes House, 88–89 Blackfriars Road, London SE1 8HA
tel. 020 7401 2077; fax 020 7633 9499
www.southwaterbooks.com; www.annesspublishing.com

If you like the images in this book and would like to investigate using them for publishing, promotions or advertising, please visit our website www.practicalpictures.com for more information.

UK agent: The Manning Partnership Ltd
tel. 01225 478444; fax 01225 478440;
sales@manning-partnership.co.uk
UK distributor: Book Trade Services; tel. 0116 2759086;
fax 0116 2759090; uksales@booktradeservices.com;
exportsales@booktradeservices.com
North American agent/distributor: National Book Network
tel. 301 459 3366; fax 301 429 5746; www.nbnbooks.com
Australian agent/distributor: Pan Macmillan Australia
tel. 1300 135 113; fax 1300 135 103;
customer.service@macmillan.com.au
New Zealand agent/distributor: David Bateman Ltd
tel. (09) 415 7664; fax (09) 415 8892

Publisher: Joanna Lorenz
Senior managing editor: Conor Kilgallon
Editors: Jennifer Mussett and Elizabeth Woodland
Photographer: Craig Robertson
Home economist: Emma MacIntosh
Stylist: Helen Trent
Designer: Nigel Partridge
Illustrator: David Cook
Production controller: Don Campaniello

© Anness Publishing Ltd 2008, 2009

Ethical Trading Policy
Because of our ongoing ecological investment programme, you, as our customer, can have the pleasure and reassurance of knowing that a tree is being cultivated on your behalf to naturally replace the materials used to make the book you are holding. For further information about this scheme, go to www.annesspublishing.com/trees

Notes
Bracketed terms are intended for American readers. For all recipes, quantities are given in both metric and imperial measures and, where appropriate, measures are also given in standard cups and spoons. Follow one set, but not a mixture, because they are not interchangeable. Standard spoon and cup measures are level. 1 tsp = 5ml, 1 tbsp = 15ml, 1 cup = 250ml/8fl oz Australian standard tablespoons are 20ml. Australian readers should use 3 tsp in place of 1 tbsp for measuring small quantities of gelatine, flour, salt etc. Medium (US large) eggs are used unless otherwise stated.

Publisher's Note
Although the advice and information in this book are believed to be accurate and true at the time of going to press, neither the authors nor the publisher can accept any legal responsibility or liability for any errors or omissions that may be made nor for any inaccuracies nor for any harm or injury that comes about from following instructions or advice in this book.

Nutritional information
The nutritional analysis given for each recipe is calculated per portion (i.e. serving or item), unless otherwise stated. If the recipe gives a range, such as Serves 4–6, then the nutritional analysis will be for the smaller portion size, i.e. 6 servings. Measurements for sodium do not include salt added to taste.

Front cover shows King Scallops with Bacon – for recipe see page 64.

Picture Acknowledgements
All pictures © Anness Publishing Ltd, except where the publisher would like to thank the following picture agencies and photographers for use of their images: Alamy Images: jacket. Arbroath Fisheries: p26 (bottom). Balvenie Distillery: p7 (bottom), p24 (bottom), p25 (top). Glenfiddich: p10 (bottom), p20 (top), and p24 (top). Glenmorangie: p25 (bottom). Loch Fyne Fisheries: p14 (top), p18 (top), p21, p23 (bottom), p27 (bottom), p34 (top and bottom), and p35 (top). MacSween of Edinburgh: p11 (top), p31 (top). Rannock Smokeries: p27 (top right). Scottish Viewpoint: p7 (top), p8 (top and bottom), p9 (bottom), p12 (top and bottom), p13 (top and bottom), p15 (top and bottom), p16 (top and bottom), p17, p19, p22 (bottom), p28 (bottom), p27 (top and bottom) p31 (bottom), p32 (bottom), p33 (top and bottom), and p35 (bottom). Uig Lodge Smoked Salmon, murdojohnsmith@gmail.com: p26 (top). VisitScotland.com: p11 (bottom), p30, p32 (top).

Previously published as part of a larger volume,
Scottish Heritage Food and Cooking.

THE FOOD AND COOKING OF
SCOTLAND

Contents

Introduction

Scotland's magnificent culinary heritage has a long and illustrious history. The heather-clad moors and dense forests that covered much of the land ensured a plentiful supply of game; the seas, rivers and lochs teemed with fish; beef, dairy cattle and sheep thrived in pastures; wild fruits, berries and aromatic herbs were gathered from fields and hedgerows; while the cold, wet climate proved ideal for oats and barley.

Below *Scotland is often carved up into three distinct areas: the rugged Highlands that dominate the northern half of the country, the bustling towns and cities of the Lowlands, and the remote, dramatic Islands that lie to the north and west.*

The flavours of Scottish cuisine to this day reflect the rugged, hardy landscape. The wild mushrooms and berries complement the rich game meats, such as venison, wild boar and grouse. The smokehouses add a sumptuous taste to salmon, trout and haddock, and have resulted in local delicacies, such as Arbroath smokies and kippers.

Scottish cuisine has undergone a major progression during the past few decades, integrating new ingredients and concepts into the traditional fare. There has been an explosion of excellent restaurants offering superb dishes using local ingredients. Cottage and artisan industries have produced a wealth of speciality foods, such as jams, cheeses and breads.

A turbulent history

Scottish cuisine has been shaped not only by geography and climate but also by various social, cultural and political events. Its development was closely interwoven with the country's turbulent history – the threads producing a rich tapestry of flavours and traditions.

Over the centuries foreign invaders and settlers, particularly those from Scandinavia, had a powerful influence on Scotland's developing cuisine. The earliest impact was from the Vikings, whose lasting contribution was to teach the Scots how to make use of the rich wealth of the seas. Trade with overseas markets through Scotland's busy ports introduced new ingredients such as spices, sugar, dried fruits and wines to the Scottish kitchen. Politics too had a major role: the Auld Alliance with France, intended to curb the dynastic ambitions of English monarchs, had a great and lasting effect on the national gastronomy. All these influences brought new foods, cooking methods, ideas and skills, which over time became part of Scottish culture. Exposure to such influences occurred throughout the country's history to result in a rich and colourful cuisine based on high-quality Scottish produce.

A harsh landscape

Scotland is well known for its dramatic mountains, lochs and beautiful scenery. The geographical differences have also had a major role in shaping Scotland's cuisine and have resulted in different regional specialities according to the particular landscape and climate. The austere, rugged grandeur of the Highlands is the natural habitat of game birds, deer, rabbits and hares. The lush fertile land of the rolling countryside of the Borders and Lowlands supports beef and dairy cattle, sheep and goats while fruit and

ATLANTIC OCEAN

Orkney Isles
Kirkwall

Shetland Isles
Lerwick

Outer Hebrides
Lewis
Stornaway
Harris
Ullapool
The Minch
Skye
Inner Hebrides

Thurso

Moray Firth

NORTH-WEST HIGHLANDS

Inverness

CAIRNGORM MTS

GRAMPIAN MOUNTAINS

Aberdeen

Mull
Oban
Iona
Jura
Islay
Arran
Firth of Clyde

Perth
Dundee

LOWLANDS
Firth of Forth

Glasgow
Edinburgh

NORTH SEA

SOUTHERN UPLANDS

THE BORDERS

Dumfries

Stranraer

Right Fishing boats bring in excellent shellfish for restaurants, seen here in Tobermory on the Isle of Mull.

berries thrive in the rich soils of Tayside and Fife. The islands, lochs and rivers are home to a flourishing fishing industry which exports fish and shellfish all over the world.

Traditional favourites

The Scots have always made the most of their natural resources and magnificent produce and are careful to preserve their time-honoured heritage dishes. Aberdeen Angus beef, Highland game, Tayside berries, salmon and other fish and shellfish and of course Scotch whisky are recognized as the finest in the world.

The old traditional favourites remain popular: haggis is still widely made and is often served with "neeps and tatties" (turnips and potatoes). In addition to national foods, every region has its own unique specialities, such as Forfar

Below The art of quality whisky making has made Scotland one of the world's leading producers.

Bridies, Selkirk bannocks, Arbroath Smokies, Loch Fyne kippers, Orkney, Islay and Galloway cheeses, Dundee cake, Moffat toffee, Edinburgh rock and a host of other delicious and much-loved delicacies that have been enjoyed for generations.

New speciality foods

A new generation of innovative and talented chefs has led something of a revolution in Scotland's restaurants, creating imaginative menus using Scottish produce, featuring many new and exciting signature dishes. Old favourites are given a modern twist and appear on many menus alongside traditional dishes. Restaurants in Edinburgh and Glasgow in particular blend Mediterranean with contemporary Scottish cuisine, and modern establishments serve dishes that fuse Middle Eastern and Far Eastern dishes with natural Scottish ingredients and flavours.

Food producers have also developed over the last decades, focusing on speciality quality foods, such as smoked salmon and whisky marmalades. Organic and free-range produce is increasing in popularity, with many farmers' markets springing up to promote cottage industries.

The first settlers

The early Neolithic settlers inhabited the land from around 4000–3000BC, coming from France and the Iberian peninsula. They cultivated cereals and used grinding stones to make flour. They fished and hunted for food, collected shellfish from the beaches, and also kept sheep, cattle and goats.

From 2500–700BC the Beaker People from Northern and Central Europe settled, bringing bronze tools and cooking pots and thereby starting Scotland's Bronze Age, altering the cooking and eating habits of the population. Their bonding into various tribes eventually formed a group known as the Picts (painted people), named by the Romans after their body paintings.

The Celts from Ireland

The Iron-Age Scot Celts came over from Ireland around 750BC. They came from today's Northern Ireland, where land shortages forced them to cross the Irish Sea to seek further pastures. The Celtic society was broken up into a caste system made up of warriors and Druids (the magicians, brehons, bards and seers), whose mystic beliefs were grounded in natural law. The Druids

Above The Neolithic settlement of Skara Brae in Orkney, where evidence of cooking and household arrangements can be seen.

performed rituals to assure the success of the hunt and the fertility of the tribe, the beasts and the land.

The Scots, as these Celts from Northern Ireland were called, brought with them the plough, horse-drawn wheeled carts and musical instruments. They lived in settlements, reared cattle

and sheep, and grew crops, most commonly oats, kale, cabbage and other hardy vegetables. Many used oats in soups and stews, and made oatcakes, which were originally cooked on hot stones and later on iron griddles (from the Gaelic *greadeal* meaning "hot stones").

The Celts left no written records but we know from ancient Roman and Greek writings that they ate little bread but great quantities of fish, meat and dairy produce. They farmed the land and grew oats, barley and vegetables such as peas, beans and cabbage, and also enjoyed wild herbs and fruits such as apples, pears, cherries and berries. They kept pigs, cattle, sheep and goats and depended on their livestock for food much more than they did their crops. Fossil records of mussel and oyster shells show that seafood was also part of their diet. The Celts roasted their food and also stewed meat and fish in pots suspended over a fire. Preservation of food was important and

Left A replica Iron-Age crannog stands on Kenmore Loch. A large family or clan would have been able to live here in times of danger, surviving on stores of dried and smoked foods.

Left Wild deer have provided an important source of nutrition since the first hunter-gatherers, and venison has become a key ingredient in Celtic and Viking recipes.

meat and fish were salted to keep during the long winter months. Wild honey was collected and used to sweeten food and also to make mead.

The Viking raids

The 9th century was characterized by numerous Viking invasions, and Scotland became a melting pot of languages, cultures and foods. The Hebrides, Orkney and Shetland were ruled by Norway for a number of centuries, with the Hebrides passing over to the Scottish crown in 1266 and Orkney and Shetland in 1472. The Norse influence remained strong and is still in evidence today, with the traditional celebrations of Yule (Christmas) and Up-Helly-Aa.

The Vikings introduced Scandinavian methods of cooking, along with the salting, smoking and curing of fish and mutton. Many foods, following their Norse origins, are dried or salted and smoked – *vivda* is wind-dried mutton,

Right The Up-Helly-Aa Viking festival at Lerwick on Shetland is a poignant link to the island's Nordic past.

dried without salt, and is served in very thin slices, and *reested* mutton (salted and smoked) is still sold by butchers in Shetland. Cabbage appears in many dishes in the Islands, as it does in Scandinavian recipes, and is eaten with pickled pork. Herring is salted, smoked and pickled and served with onions, as it is prepared in Scandinavia.

The Scots' fondness for fish, particularly in the Northern Isles, can

partly be attributed to the Vikings, and their influence has not only survived in fish dishes but is also evident in other recipes, such as *fricadellans* (meatballs) from the Scandinavian *frikadeller*. Liver *muggies* (fish stomachs stuffed with seasoned fish livers) are derived from the Old Norse *magi*.

The Viking tradition of eating out of wooden bowls and plates with a sharp pointed knife was also adopted. Spoons were made from wood, horn or animal bone and were frequently carved with intricate patterns and the heads of fabulous beasts. Similarly, lavishly decorated horns were used to serve drinks and soups.

The Vikings were great drinkers, and brought with them a number of flavoursome concoctions. *Whipkull*, an ancient festive drink of eggs and sugar whisked over heat, is identical to the Norwegian *eggedosis*, the national festive dessert served with crisp biscuits. It is also similar to an Icelandic soup.

The clan system

Key to Scottish cuisine is the illustrious history of the clans and clan culture. The system is believed to have been founded by a group of Scots who settled on the west coast of Scotland in the 6th century. The word clan is directly drawn from the Gaelic word *clann*, meaning children. The clans were made up of both "native men" (with a direct blood relationship with their chief and with each other) and "broken men" from other clans, who sought the protection of the clan. Many clan names begin with "Mac", which means "son of".

The clan chieftain shared his home with relatives and clanspeople, who were employed by him in return for their keep. The rule of the chief over his lands was virtually autonomous, but there were frequent feuds between the clans and battles were common. Stronger, larger clans predominated, with Clan Donald reputed to be the most powerful.

Tartan became an important symbol of clan kinship amongst the Highlanders and each clan developed its own tartan

Below *Whisky was originally made by clans, and the quality and flavour was symbolic of the clan's status.*

Above *Highland cows were reared by the clans for beef and dairy products.*

for identification and to depict the prestige of the clan. It was worn at feasts and clan celebrations.

It was a matter of pride and honour for the clan chief to offer his very best food and drink to visitors. Reports from travellers in the 18th century praised the generous hospitality they received from the clans in the Highlands. A breakfast of porridge (oatmeal) was typically accompanied by fresh cream, eggs, cheese, bannocks and oatcakes and was washed down with milk, buttermilk, ale or whisky. A special

drink for honoured guests was Auld Man's Milk – eggs, milk, honey and whisky beaten together.

Sir Walter Scott described the 14th-century funeral feast of a Highland chief in *The Fair Maid of Perth* (1828): "... Pits wrought in the hillside and lined with heated stones, served for stewing immense quantities of beef, mutton and venison; wooden spits supported sheep and goats, which were roasted entire; others were cut into joints and seethed in cauldrons made of the animals' own skins, sewed hastily together and filled with water; while huge quantities of pike, trout, salmon and char were broiled with more ceremony on glowing embers."

Clan repression

During the 18th century, the English government was determined to curtail the power of the Highland chiefs and prevent uprisings. They built roads in the previously inaccessible Highlands, and cleared much of the land (along with the Highland families) to make way for sheep farming and gaming

estates. The draconian Act of Proscription (1747) made it illegal to wear Highland dress (except in the military), and banned the use of clan names, celebrations and music.

The Highland Clearances had great repercussions for the Highlanders. Their self-sufficiency, which had relied on wild game and produce from cows, sheep, goats and hens, disappeared and they were left destitute. Many were evicted without their possessions, not even cooking utensils, as they surveyed their burning homes and lands. A few sympathetic English landlords distributed food to the stricken Highlanders, but it wasn't enough and thousands emigrated to the New World in search of a better life. The emptiness of the Highlands today is a lasting reminder of those terrible times.

The clans and other Scots attempted to bring the Stewart kings back to the throne; these episodes became known as the Jacobite Rebellions. In 1746, the "Young Pretender" or Bonnie Prince

Right Bagpipes, tartan and traditional clan celebrations can now be found throughout Scotland.

Charlie was defeated at the Battle of Culloden. The clan lands were confiscated, and Jacobite supporters were imprisoned – including Rob Roy MacGregor. Bonnie Prince Charlie escaped and was helped to Skye by Flora Macdonald, who disguised Charlie as her maid for the crossing.

Revival of the clans

Tartan made a welcome return in 1782 when the Highland regiments, such as the Black Watch, were permitted to wear a regimental tartan. The Highlanders became keen to re-establish (or in some cases re-invent) their family tartans and celebrate their clan culture. Queen Victoria, who loved all things Scottish, encouraged the use of tartan and interest spread. Today, especially with the energy that has

come from the new Scottish Parliament, the clans are celebrated, and many traditions, foods and festivals enjoyed throughout the country.

Below The Highland Games re-create the clan competitiveness through games such as the tug o' war.

Foreign influences

Scottish cooking has absorbed many fascinating culinary influences throughout history, as a result of foreign invaders, settlers and traders. New ingredients, recipes and cooking methods have been introduced, all of which have had a huge impact on the Scottish kitchen and the way that food is enjoyed.

The Auld Alliance

One of the biggest influences on the Scottish kitchen was the Auld Alliance. From 1295 Scotland and France united against English invaders in an alliance that lasted 233 years. James V married the French Mary of Guise, mother of Mary Queen of Scots. The latter lived at the French court and married the future Francis II of France. The widowed Mary of Guise ruled Scotland until her daughter returned in 1561 after the death of her husband. Recipes of the time owed much to the French, who came over during the Auld Alliance. The French influence remains today in many words in common use: *ashet* – a large serving dish from the French *assiette*; *hotch potch* – vegetable soup from the

Above *The French influence is seen in many grand estates, such as in Bowhill House in the Borders, built in 1795.*

French *hochepot*; and a rich bread pudding that dates back to the 13th century called *pampurdy*, a corruption of *pain perdue*, which means smothered bread.

It was during the Auld Alliance that dessert was introduced for the first time. After the main meal the table was disserved (cleared), fruits and

Left *French monks left their mark in the 13th-century Beauly Priory.*

The origin of Drambuie

When Bonnie Prince Charlie was in hiding after Culloden, he was taken from Skye to the mainland by a man named MacKinnon. As a reward, the prince gave him the recipe for his own liqueur, created for him when he was at the French court. It was called, in Gaelic, *An Dram Buidheach* (the drink that satisfies). The MacKinnon clan made some each year, solely for their own use. In the 1870s, John Ross, the owner of the Broadford Inn on Skye, persuaded the MacKinnons to make large quantities of the liqueur so he could sell it. In 1893 John Ross's son, James, patented the name Drambuie as a trademark.

sweetmeats were eaten in another room. It was another 50 years before this custom was adopted in England.

Many dishes in French and Scottish cooking became closely related. In Scottish towns professional bakers, known as baxters (the original meaning

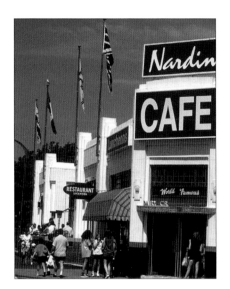

Above An Italian ice cream parlour built in Art-Deco style in Largs on the coast of Ayrshire.

of the word baxter was a female cook), used French methods and recipes. The bakers were patronized by the wealthy who could afford the best ingredients such as wheat flour and sugar. It was said that only French and Viennese bakers surpassed those of Edinburgh.

Later still, after the French Revolution in 1789 when many French chefs fled to Scotland, it became fashionable for wealthy Scots and the nobility to boast of employing a French chef and thus encouraging French cuisine.

The Dutch influence

Trade with Holland in the 16th and 17th centuries led to the introduction of Dutch recipes, which were integrated into the Scottish kitchen. These took advantage of the dried fruits and spices that had arrived on the ships of the Dutch East India Company. In Scotland a plain, yeasted bun is known as a cookie and the name probably comes from the Dutch *koek*, or cake. Aberdeen *crullas* are delicious sweet fried cakes and their name possibly comes from the Dutch *krullen* (to curl).

Italian cuisine

In the 19th century many Italian immigrants arrived in search of a better life and brought their culinary traditions to Scotland. Most opened restaurants and cafés. They soon realized that most Scottish people had only basic cooking facilities and worked long hours. This led some Italians to sell ready-made foods such as hot peas and, later, fish and chips, unwittingly creating the thriving take-away culture that is such a feature of Scottish cities today. Other immigrants sold home-made ice cream and it was these immigrants who introduced ice cream as a street food, selling it from gaily painted carts and crying out "*Gelati, ecco un poco!*" which is why they became known as "hokey pokey men" and the ice cream they sold was called "hokey pokey". Some sold both – hot food in winter and ice cream in summer. Their hard work paid off and by the 1920s many could afford to abandon their small shops in poorer areas and open luxurious establishments in fashionable areas such as Sauchiehall Street in Glasgow. These establishments

increased in popularity and quickly expanded into cafés with full meals on the menu. Similar cafés were opened by Italians throughout Scotland and records show that, in 1904, the number of cafés in Glasgow alone had doubled from the previous year. The cafés became popular meeting places, especially for the young, particularly as they were among the few places that opened on Sundays.

Today many of Scotland's Italian restaurants retain their impressive reputation for quality and tradition, with many coming under the umbrella of Ciao Italia, founded in 1982. This organisation is responsible for maintaining and building on the values of Italian cuisine abroad.

Scots-Italians continue to run award-winning shops and restaurants. Their role in influencing Scottish eating styles continues today. Ice cream and fish and chips, known as a "fish supper", are an indispensable part of Scottish food and eateries.

Below Italian meets Scottish: second- and third-generation Italians have opened restaurants in Edinburgh.

Life in the Highlands

Even before the suppression of the clans and the Clearances, life in the Highlands was bleak. The clans dominated the hardy lands, making the most of wild game and dairy products from their herds of Highland cattle.

Broths and soups were the staple dishes, providing the main meal of the day for many. They would simmer in a cauldron set over a peat fire throughout the day, with wild herbs (especially young, tender nettle leaves) added for flavour. The Highlanders ate little in the way of green vegetables, preferring boiled nettles instead, which are a natural blood purifier and contain useful amounts of iron and vitamins A and C. A few vegetables, such as kail (or kale), onions and leeks, were cultivated in the kailyard (a piece of land next to the house set aside as a sort of kitchen garden), and most of these ended up in the soup pot.

Berries and wild fruits were eaten with cream or soft cheese. Before sugar was widely available, honey was the main sweetener and boys were sent out to collect wild honey. Heather honey is

Above *The rivers and lochs have always provided an abundance of foods, notably salmon.*

a Scottish speciality and is a rich reddish-brown colour, with a dense texture and distinctive flavour. This is one of nature's last truly wild and unadulterated foods.

Every summer the cattle were moved to the mountain pastures and the women and children went with them to live in basic huts known as shielings. The women made butter and cheese from the milk of cows, sheep and goats. Butter was salted so that it would keep for use over the winter. Another traditional way of preserving butter was to bury it in a peat bog, and examples of bog butter are sometimes found today, including a 2,000-year-old specimen that is now in the Museum of Scotland in Edinburgh.

Occasionally domesticated animals were slaughtered for fresh meat. This was enjoyed in celebration feasts or was sometimes salted to preserve it for the harsh winter months. The main meats were mutton or beef as the Highlanders held pork in disdain. Food was frequently given to the clan chief in lieu of rent.

Left *Survival in the Highlands relied upon wild deer to provide venison as a delicious and nutritious food source.*

The Clearances and the crofters

The Highlands changed radically following the dramatic defeat at Culloden in 1746. Where once the clans had dominated the wilderness, power passed into the hands of lairds placed by the king to control the wayward Highlanders. Highland culture, language and even dress were suppressed for years to come and the old traditional Highland way of life disappeared, never to return. Poverty and hardship led to the emigration of thousands of Scots during the time that became known as the Clearances, many boarding ships bound for America.

The Agricultural Revolution during the latter part of the 18th century and into the 19th century led to a change in the landscape. The great forests that covered the Highlands were cleared away within a space of 20 years.

The gradual development of agriculture and the destruction of woods and forests led to the near extinction of many wild animals previously hunted for food. The wild boar, elk and bears that had roamed the forests in the early period eventually died out as their natural habitat was destroyed. Deer, that had previously inhabited the forests, moved up into the hills and adapted their original diet of young tree shoots to heather.

Sheep replaced people, as land was combined into huge farming estates for the king's favourites. These landowning gentry allowed the peasants to work smallholdings, a practice known as the crofting system.

Above The picturesque fishing village of Plockton was once a Gaelic-speaking community surviving on traditional fishing and crofting.

Left Crofting cottages still exist today, with the stone house at the top of a strip of land used to supply oats, vegetables and dairy produce.

Above *A replica interior of a crofter's cottage, with the fire for cooking in the centre of the room.*

The crofters lived in small stone houses with roofs of wood and thatch. Farm animals, such as poultry, lived in one end of the building and the family at the other. A peat fire burned continuously in the middle of the room, where food was cooked in an iron pot suspended from the ceiling. There were no windows, but a hole in the roof allowed the smoke to escape. They were often referred to as blackhouses as the interiors were black with smoke.

The crofters' diet consisted mainly of cheese, butter, herbs, seasonal fruits and vegetables, porridge, oatcakes and barley bannocks. A bowl of steaming hot porridge (oatmeal) served with thick cold fresh cream provided a sustaining and nourishing breakfast. A pot of broth often thickened with oatmeal and flavoured with wild herbs simmered all day over the fire for the evening meal, accompanied by soft barley bannocks cooked on a bakestone or girdle (griddle). A piece of mutton or venison provided a welcome addition to the pot. Filling staples were potatoes and oatmeal boiled in water (*brochan*) and meals were accompanied by milk,

buttermilk, ale or whisky. In the summer wild berries and fruits were enjoyed with cream and honey.

There are around 17,000 crofts today and most of them now have modern amenities. Crofting has undergone a revival and has seen the re-emergence of traditional cottage industries.

The gaming estates

Hunting was a popular sport with the nobility in the 18th and 19th centuries, many of whom travelled up from England. Large gaming estates began to

appear, the later ones becoming more flamboyant and luxurious. Every laird, as lords were known in Scotland, owned dovecotes for pigeons, and huge flocks of wild pigeons also thrived in Scotland. They provided fresh meat in winter.

Increasingly tight laws were put in place to prevent the locals from hunting and fishing, yet poaching increased as they considered that wild animals and fish could not be regarded as property – they belonged to no one and were there for the taking.

Deer and boar were hunted on horseback with dogs. A more formal hunt was the drive, where beaters drove the game to within the hunters' range. In the murky peat bogs the *tinchel* method developed. Walls of stone or brush were built on either side of a glen, and men on foot drove the deer from the hills into the enclosure.

Every part of the deer was used; even the antlers which provided deerhorn jelly. Venison was usually roasted and tougher cuts were stewed or used to fill pasties. Venison collops, a very old dish, was made with thick steaks from the

Below *Elaborate hunting lodges still host gaming parties with traditional hunting and banquets.*

boned haunch. Deer haggis used the heart and liver and the liver was also eaten on its own. Deer tripe (*pocha buidh* or yellow bag) was another speciality. Deer puddings were made from deer suet mixed with oatmeal and onions put into cleaned deerskins and boiled. Venison was usually served with a claret sauce or gravy.

In the late 18th century hunting methods changed radically when improved firearms removed the need for dogs. Many landowners rented out land for deer stalking. These "shooting lets" were advertised in newspapers and the thrill of hunting proved popular, despite the fact that there was no accommodation and often no roads. By the mid-19th century hunting was a fashionable pastime. Queen Victoria and Prince Albert endorsed the new vogue for hunting when they bought Balmoral, giving Albert land on which to hunt and fish while the Queen sketched and took the bracing Scottish air. Queen Victoria was very fond of game dishes, especially pheasant and woodcock stuffed with truffles, foie gras and herbs.

Hunting and fishing today

Today syndicates own many of the large estates and rent out the shooting rights. Game birds are bred to be shot for sport and for the table. Game, fish and wildfowl are protected and can only be hunted at certain times of the year, to allow stocks to be replenished.

Grouse shoots are especially popular and attract people from all over the world. The Glorious Twelfth is the start of the grouse-shooting season on 12 August, ending on 10 December. Feasts are enjoyed with tables filled with lavishly decorated game meats.

Consumption of farmed venison is increasing as more people recognize the benefits of eating this low-fat, tasty meat. Wild venison may sometimes

come from old, tougher animals, or may not have been hung for sufficient time and so have little flavour. Farmed venison on the other hand has consistency of flavour and texture and needs no marinating. Many venison farms encourage visitors.

Scotland's salmon and trout rivers such as the Tay, the Dee, the Spey and the Tweed are well-stocked and offer unrivalled pleasure for keen anglers.

Tourism and Highland activities

There has been a surge in tourism over the last few decades, and this sector today accounts for many businesses in the Highlands. Many

Above *Hunting continues to be popular in Scotland, although today it is heavily regulated to protect species and the local ecosystem.*

excellent restaurants, hotels, guesthouses, visitor centres, ancestral homes and castles have opened. Mountaineering, sailing, walking, skiing (in winter) and sporting estates attract keen sportsmen from around the globe.

There is plenty for the food-loving tourist – you can watch traditional sweets (candies) being made, or visit an oat mill, shortbread bakery or whisky distillery and of course the region's restaurants, pubs and hotels offer a selection of tasty local specialities.

Life on the Islands

The remote Scottish Islands are a world of breathtaking scenery. However, any view of a coastal cottage or village with a backdrop of towering mountains brings home the sheer isolation and struggle for existence here. Amongst the extraordinarily beautiful and dramatic lochs and massive mountains, livings are made from patches of fertile soil and the fruitful lochs and seas.

The Northern Isles (called Nordereys by the Norsemen), Orkney and Shetland, have had ties with Scandinavia since Viking times, whereas the Western Isles are mainly Celt-influenced. Piracy and smuggling were a part of life, with the latter providing a good income. Influences from shipwrecked and smuggled goods from abroad took hold. Fair Isle in Shetland gave its name to the multi-coloured knitting designs which were probably copied from the clothing worn by those shipwrecked in the 1588 Spanish Armada catastrophe.

The Western Isles off the north-west coast of Scotland include the Inner and Outer Hebrides. The Inner Hebrides are closer to the mainland and include Skye, Jura and Islay, and the sub-group of the Small Isles, such as Eigg and

Rhum. The more remote Outer Hebrides include Lewis and Harris.

Fish and shellfish have always been the staple diet on all the islands, eaten alone or made into nourishing soups, stews and pies. Seaweed collected from the shores is often cooked and eaten as a vegetable, as well as being used as fertilizer, and the ashes from burnt seaweed were once used instead of salt to preserve cheese.

Above As for most islands, fishing is the main source of income on the Isle of Lewis in the Outer Hebrides.

The culture of both groups of islands is distinct from that of the mainland and their remoteness has served to preserve their unique traditions.

The Shetland Isles and Orkney

The Vikings made the Northern Islands of Shetland and Orkney their home, and the islands still celebrate their Norse way of life. Gaelic was never commonly used, and many places still have Norse names. Christmas is known by its Norwegian name of Yule, the ancient feast of the winter solstice.

The Shetland Isles, a group of over 100 islands, were once part of the Danish kingdom. The culture, traditions and dialect still have a strong Scandinavian flavour. The peat-covered hills contrast with the green arable land of Orkney. Sheep are raised in Shetland,

Left Cows produce fine dairy foods and now support a thriving ice cream industry on Orkney.

Above *The familiar sight of a fishing boat entering the harbour of the busy fishing town of Lerwick on the remote Shetland Isles.*

but there is little agriculture; it is fishing that is most important to the islands' economy.

The most important industry has always been the deep-sea fishing for ling and cod. This was known as the *haaf*, carried out from May to August. It was a dangerous and arduous occupation, and many boats were tragically lost. By the 18th century dried ling had become a major export.

Shetlanders, like Scandinavians, are very fond of fermented fish and make use of the heads, roes and livers of white fish discarded from the salting process. Fish livers were also melted down and the oil was used in lamps.

Oats and barley are grown along with some vegetables. Livestock provides meat, milk, cheese and butter. A local wind-dried meat, such as pork, mutton or beef, is known as *vivda*. Salted and spiced minced (ground) beef is called *sassermaet* and is used to make patties called *bröenies*.

Orkney comprises more than 70 islands (only 17 are inhabited). Its name is believed to come from the Icelandic *Orkneyjar*, or Seal Islands. Orkney has more farmland than Shetland, with oats and barley as the main crops. Potatoes are cultivated in the peaty soil and damp climate. Kale flourishes and used to be preserved in barrels with fat and oatmeal. The dairy industry produces famous cheeses, cream and, more recently, ice cream. Cheeses used to be buried in oatmeal to keep them fresh, although it was more usual to eat

cheese young and fresh. Cattle are also farmed for beef. High-quality organic salmon are farmed in vast sea pens off Orkney and have paler, less fatty flesh than ordinary farmed salmon.

Early daily fare in the Orkneys included a morning piece of half a bannock made from bere. Traditional oatmeal gingerbread is Orkney *broonie* – the name derives from the Norse *bruni*, meaning a thick bannock. Sour skons made with buttermilk are popular, sometimes flavoured with caraway seeds.

The Western Isles

On the farthest edge of Europe lie the Western Isles, many of them mountainous and infertile. In winter the weather is harsh with strong Atlantic winds and heavy rain, although snow is rare. The summer is generally warm and

Left Coopers repair casks ready for use: the islands of the Inner Hebrides are famed for their fine single malt and blended whiskies.

by the Norsemen until it passed to the Scottish crown in 1226. Both Celtic and Norse traditions are strong and about half the population speaks Gaelic.

Sheep, wool, cattle and fishing are the chief sources of income, together with a growing tourist industry. Foods include locally made cheeses and seafood, including scallops, lobster, oysters, langoustines, cod, haddock, mackerel, and wild salmon and trout. Talisker, one of the world's great malt whiskies, is produced here and the brewery makes superb ales using only natural ingredients.

The Isle of Islay is famed for its whisky distilleries, producing some of the best whiskies in the world. Many of the distilleries date back to the 17th and 18th centuries, competing with each other to improve quality and flavour over the years.

Below European lobsters, as found in the seas around Scotland, are highly prized. Lobster fishing is a good source of income for the islanders on Mull.

it stays light until about midnight. Gaelic culture is dominant in the islands, and they remain the only place in Scotland where the language is spoken on a daily basis.

Religion is largely Free Presbyterianism and Sunday is strictly kept as the Sabbath, with no work taking place. Some of the other islands are mainly Roman Catholic, as their remoteness shielded them from the Scottish Reformation. A strongly held religion helped many communities survive the hardships experienced on the remote islands.

Whilst many of the Hebrides, such as Skye, have become successful tourist centres, others, such as the remote St Kilda, are now uninhabited.

The Inner Hebrides

These comprise the great swathe of islands lying off the western coast of Scotland – east of the Outer Hebrides, Skye southwards to the Kintyre

peninsula. Each is very different in appearance and atmosphere, with its own distinct culture.

One of the most accessible of the islands is Mull, with its idyllic fishing port Tobermory drawing in tourists – now the mainstay of the economy. Fishing, especially for lobsters, is still a good source of income for the islanders. Close by is tiny Iona, one of the most important religious sites in Europe, and still a Roman Catholic pilgrimage site. Nearby, the dramatic uninhabited island of Staffa, looms out of the sea like a great cathedral of natural basalt columns. It was the inspiration for Mendelssohn's *Hebrides Overture*. Seals, whales and porpoise follow the fishing boats as they head out.

The beautiful Isle of Skye attracts tourists from all over the world to see the incredible landscapes and enjoy the local festivals. It was dominated by the Celts until the 8th century, then ruled

The Outer Hebrides

A long strand of islands and islets, the Outer Hebrides lie west of the mainland. Relentlessly battered by fierce Atlantic winds, they pose a bleak and hostile environment for human life, with heather, bog and few trees. The landscape is dominated by rock and there are freshwater and sea lochs. Shellfish abound and live seafood is exported worldwide. The finest lobsters go to the best restaurants in Edinburgh, London and Paris. Shops and restaurants on the islands sell a stunning variety of fish and shellfish, both fresh and smoked.

Sheep and beef cattle are kept. The crofters used to grow potatoes and a few other vegetables on the hillsides, fertilizing the meagre soil with seaweed, but today fruit, vegetables and grains are brought across from the mainland.

The most famous products of the islands are the tweeds. Harris Tweed is world-renowned and is an important industry. Although there are now larger manufacturers, many weavers still work from home or small workshops.

Other high-quality traditional products are also made here, such as the fine smoked salmon from the Isle of Lewis, as well as some excellent local cheeses and preserves.

St Kilda is the most remote and hostile group of Scottish Islands. St Kilda was inhabited until 1930, the islanders scraping a living mostly from fish, shellfish and sea birds such as puffins, fulmar and Solan goose (or gannet) and their eggs. The sea birds also provided feathers for eiderdowns, and oil that was used for lamps.

Solan goose was a speciality, eaten fresh or preserved. The plucked and cleaned birds were lightly salted then hung in small peat huts called *stypes*, with open ends so the birds dried in the cold dry winds. These wind-blown or blawn birds were sometimes stored in beehive-shaped earth cells called *cleits*. The cooked bird was known in Gaelic as a *guga* and was reputed to have a delicate flavour, not at all fishy or strong.

In the mid-19th century steamships provided more contact with the outside world. During World War I a garrison was stationed on the main island, but when the regular deliveries of mail and food stopped after the war the islanders felt very isolated. Food shortages ensued and this, together with the emigration of many young islanders, eventually led to a request for evacuation to the mainland, where they had to adjust their eating habits, occupations and entire lifestyles.

***Below** The shores provide plenty of foods for foraging, such as cockles and mussels and the tasty seaweeds.*

Life in the Lowlands

The lush pastures of the Lowlands stand in contrast with the rugged Highlands. They produce much of the dairy products, fruit, vegetables and grains that are consumed in Scotland.

Fishing and farming were the main sources of food in the Lowlands for thousands of years. Sheep were kept mainly for wool and milk, and pigs provided bacon and pork. Cows were kept for beef and dairy produce. Lowlanders grew grains and vegetables in their kailyards, usually bere (a type of barley), oats, beans, peas and kale – Scotland's national green vegetable. In the 18th century, the kail bell was rung at two o'clock to signal the main meal of the day.

Below The city of Edinburgh was one of the most developed cities in Europe by the 18th century, with plentiful food provided by the surrounding lowlands.

Bannocks were usually made with barley, often mixed with peasemeal, oats and rye, when they were known as *meslin* (mixed) bannocks. Rich Scotch ale was the preferred drink.

Fishing in sea, river and loch

Around the coast fishing was a major source of income. Ancient picturesque fishing villages such as St Monans, Anstruther and Pittenweem (the latter holds an annual fish festival) were once thriving seaports and still sell sparklingly fresh fish and shellfish. Musselburgh, a few miles from Edinburgh, was the site of an important Roman camp and its name comes from the famous mussel bed. Mussels are still enjoyed there today.

Salmon smoking and pickling were important industries in Scotland as early as the 13th century. The River Tay in Fife is renowned as one of the best salmon rivers in Britain. Glasgow was known as a salmon fishing village and the River Clyde was once a famous salmon river. The fishing rights were eagerly sought and were mentioned in charters of the 12th century. By the 18th century, enormous catches of salmon meant that it was cheap. Farm workers even stipulated in their contracts that salmon was to be served only three times a week. Today there are no salmon in the Clyde due to overfishing and pollution.

Sugar and sweets

By the 18th century, Glasgow had become the largest importer of sugar in Britain. Glaswegians became fond of making sweets and the famous Scots sweet tooth developed. The women who made and sold toffee were known as Sweetie Wives.

Above *Toffees and fudges are a speciality in Glasgow, Britain's largest sugar port.*

Every town developed its own unique sweets. The now world-famous, pastel-coloured, powdery Edinburgh rock was discovered by accident by a young sweetmaker called Sandy Ferguson, also known as "Sweetie Sandy", who went on to produce it in a grand scale. *Soor plooms* from Galashiels are round green sweets with an acid tang, believed to commemorate the day when a gang of English marauders was overcome after being caught unawares as they feasted on unripe plums. Jethart snails are dark peppermint-flavoured toffees, introduced by a French prisoner from the Napoleonic Wars. *Gundy* is an old-fashioned toffee, originally made and sold by a Mrs Flockhart in Potter Row in Edinburgh. Gold-striped Moffat Toffee is still made today in the town after which it is named and has an unusual sherbet tang. Treacle candy was a farmhouse sweet, made using the molasses kept on farms for mixing with the cattle mash.

In rural areas it was the custom for lads and lassies to meet in the evening in someone's house for sweet-making. Everyone had great fun, and the evening would usually end with dancing and merriment.

Above *Shortbreads and sweet biscuits are often topped with local berries, such as strawberries and raspberries.*

A wealth of food and drink

At the beginning of the 18th century there were approximately one million people living in Scotland and 90 per cent of these lived in small settlements and communities. Developments in agriculture and improved transport resulted in the emergence of heavy industries in towns and cities, with the result that Scotland became one of the most industrialized countries in Europe.

A decline in manufacturing in the latter part of the 20th century has led to the emphasis shifting back to food. The staple industries of the Lowlands are now fishing and farming. The fertile farmland of the Lowlands supports grain crops as well as beef and dairy cattle. The cool summers and long hours of daylight result not only in Britain's finest sweet luscious raspberries, but also gooseberries, blackcurrants, strawberries, tayberries and blackberries, which are all grown commercially in the region.

The seaside coastal towns and ports are home to busy fish markets and smokeries. The fishing ports of Macduff, Fraserburgh and Peterhead (Europe's largest fishing port) share a rich history. Buckie proudly displays its fishing heritage in a new visitor centre.

Lowland whiskies such as Auchentoshan Littlemill, Rosebank and Bladnoch are softer than those of the Highlands and Islands and can be a more gentle introduction to drinking malt whisky.

Below *The rich pastures in the central valleys provide excellent cheeses and other dairy products.*

The Scotch whisky distilleries

Ask people what they associate most with Scotland and you'll probably get a variety of answers – tartan, golf and Robbie Burns would certainly all be mentioned. But the most common answer is likely to be whisky.

Acknowledged as Scotland's national drink, whisky – in the Gaelic, *uisge beatha* (pronounced oosh-ga bah-hah), meaning water of life – has been produced here for centuries as a way of using up rain-soaked barley after a wet harvest. The whisky industry has now grown into one of the country's biggest earners, bringing in hundreds of millions of pounds annually.

During the 17th century the popularity of whisky grew steadily and many distilleries sprang up to meet increasing demand. However the finest whiskies were those distilled by the Highland chiefs for their own households, although these gradually died out with the clans.

The British Government imposed a tax on malt whisky in 1713, to the outrage of Scotland. So began the era of illicit stills and smuggling. Raids by excise men and their attempts to close down the illegal stills failed and the defiant Highlanders continued to distil whisky in huge quantities. This was smuggled into the Lowlands and England by a variety of ingenious methods, and outwitting the excise men became a way of life. One of the greatest smugglers was Helen Cumming, the wife of John who founded the Cardhu distillery in Morayshire.

Eventually Alexander, Duke of Gordon, persuaded the British Government to see the folly of its ways and in 1823 an act was passed permitting licensed distilling. Small private stills were still illegal so the practice of whisky-making in the home ceased almost completely. However this encouraged the production of whisky on a large scale and distilleries were set up in areas where the natural conditions were favourable. George Smith – a previously illicit distiller and smuggler – opened the first licensed distillery on Speyside.

Above The popularity of whisky gained momentum through the 19th century and spread to England.

The processes

Single malt whisky is made from malted barley in pot stills. Barley is soaked for two days then spread out on the malting floor for about ten days to germinate, when the starch converts to sugar. Then it is spread out on the perforated kiln floor, with a peat furnace beneath, to halt the germination process. Once dried the malt is ground into grist then mixed with hot water in a mash tun. The resulting sugary liquid, wort, is drawn off and the solids are used for cattle feed. The wort is cooled and poured into washbacks, yeast is added and fermentation begins. After two days wash, a weak form of alcohol, develops. It is from this that the spirit is produced.

Malt whisky is distilled twice, or perhaps three times. This involves a process of heating and cooling, evaporation and condensation. The

Left A worker turns the grain on the floor of a malting house to encourage germination.

first distillate, the low wines, is distilled again. After this it is a matter of the expert eye of the stillman to make sure everything goes to plan. Then water is added and the spirit is sealed in casks and stored for at least three years. Single malt whisky is left much longer for its complex character to develop. When they have reached the end of their useful lives – filled three or four times – the casks are broken up and used for smoking salmon.

In 1830 the manufacture of whisky was revolutionized by the invention of the patent still. This could produce alcohol much more cheaply than the old pot still. The Highland distillers were outraged and argued that the new product was "Scotch'd Spirit" and most definitely not whisky. The patent still did not rely on the correct climate, peat and water, and used malted and unmalted barley mashed to produce a "grain" whisky unlike malt whisky.

Below Copper pot stills have been used in Scotland since the 1500s.

Some distillers began experimenting with blends of both malt and grain whisky and from 1860 the Excise permitted the blending of whiskies from different distilleries. Skilful blending created distinctive brands, which were uniform and unchanging in character, and by the mid-19th century, patent still distillers such as Tommy Dewar were

Above The casks are carefully constructed from oak, imparting the wood flavour to the whisky.

established. Sales of both types of whisky soared in Scotland and by the end of the 19th century the English had been won over too.

Whisky-making today

Scotland continues to produce outstanding malt, grain and blended whiskies. Many of the best-known quality distilleries are still owned by the family or clan that began making the whisky centuries before. Very often these distilleries compete with one another, especially those in the same region, continually pushing up the standards and improving the flavours of their products. The traditional methods are retained as much as possible, while taking advantage of the new techniques and machinery.

The distilleries have benefited from new markets. These have come from the surge in international exports and also from many Scottish food and drink manufacturers who now add whisky to many high-quality products to enhance the flavour.

The smokehouses

Smoked foods have been enjoyed since antiquity, and smoking, particularly of fish, has been practised throughout Scotland since the Iron Age. Foods were salted, and then hung in huts and caves where smoke from the cooking fires pervaded the fish or meat. It was discovered that the tarry substances in wood-smoke killed bacteria and formed an impervious layer on the surface of the food, which preserved it. The smoke also penetrated the food imparting the characteristic rich, smoky flavour. Foods were heavily smoked and salted to preserve them for the lean winter months. Smoking was also used to preserve fish that needed to be transported to the mainland or abroad.

Fresh fish such as haddock were heavily salted, then smoked for up to three weeks. Salmon was also smoked, but the end result was hard and salty – very different from the tender, mild product we know today. The famous Arbroath smokies are haddock that

Below Smoking haddock is still very much a cottage industry in Arbroath, with a designated area of the town set aside to protect the old industry.

have been dry-salted, tied in pairs then hot smoked to a rich copper colour, leaving the insides creamy white. They are still made in a number of family-run smokehouses around Arbroath harbour.

Smokehouses were built in coastal areas, where fish were smoked as they came ashore. Early smokehouses were simple wood or brick buildings fitted with beams, across which lengths of wood were balanced for hanging the fish. Fishwives gutted, split, cleaned and salted the fish and laid the fires in the smokehouses. They also smoked their own fish over peat in their home chimneys – a practice which was common throughout Scotland until the mid-19th century.

Scotland's oldest smoking house still stands on River Ugie in Peterhead. Built in 1585 for the Fifth Earl of Marischal to store his fish and game, the tiny building still has the original 16th-century scarf joints on the ceiling beams. Locally caught wild salmon and trout are still smoked here, along with top-quality farmed salmon from Orkney.

Fish was not the only food to be smoked. Women in the Highlands and Islands smoked home-made sausages in

Above High-quality smoked salmon is filleted by hand before smoking.

their chimneys. Geese were also sometimes cured and smoked. Joints of beef and mutton hams (legs of mutton cured and smoked in the same way as hams) were much sought after in the 18th century, enjoying a large export market to the New World and the West Indies. Smoking continued in much the same way until 1939, when the Torry Research Station in Aberdeen developed the Torry kiln. This was a new controlled smoking kiln, which produced a uniform product of a high quality. The process was achieved using a forced draught, which improved the drying and smoking. The fish were exposed to moderate temperatures (prime for bacterial growth) for a shorter period. The result was that more fish could be processed in a shorter time and to a higher quality.

The smoking process

The smoking process involves first curing by dry-salting, brining or marinating (according to the producer), then air-drying the food before smoking. The cure is a major factor in

Above *Whole fish, such as herring, are delicious smoked, making popular breakfast dishes.*

Above *Thinly sliced smoked salmon is soft and tender, with a delicate and subtle smoky flavour.*

Above *Smoked venison and other types of meat and game are becoming increasingly popular.*

the flavour of the food and many producers have their own particular curing recipes, which may include herbs, spices, brown sugar, whisky and molasses. The choice of wood greatly contributes to the taste of the finished product. Oak and beech are very popular as they impart a delicate nutty taste, and sometimes a small amount of aromatic wood such as juniper is added towards the end of smoking for an extra-special flavour.

Today food is smoked more for its flavour than for preservation. Although commercial smokehouses have large, specially constructed kilns, Scotland retains many traditional small-scale smokehouses using time-honoured methods of filleting, salting and smoking – a skilled craft that is difficult to achieve in large-scale smokehouses. The excellent quality and flavour of foods smoked by traditional methods speak for themselves.

Smoked salmon from Scotland is internationally renowned for its quality, texture and flavour. Other meats, such as hams, bacon, venison and poultry, are popular smoked foods today, as is cheese. Enterprising Scottish specialist smokers now even produce smoked alligator, kangaroo and ostrich.

Below *Organic salmon and mussel farms at Loch Fyne produce high-quality smoked and cured goods.*

The king of fish – salmon

The wild salmon is a magnificent creature. The skin of its sleek, muscular body shimmers silver, while its deep pink-red flesh is rich and full of flavour. The flavour and texture of wild Scottish salmon (*Salmo salar*) surpasses that of all other varieties, and it is eagerly sought after by gourmets. Keen anglers from all over the world will happily pay vast sums for the privilege of fishing for this superb fish.

Salmon in the wild

Salmon make the exhausting journey from the North Atlantic Ocean back to the river of their birth to breed. This is the best time to catch them, as their flavour and texture are at their finest – they have eaten heavily from the rich feeding grounds of the ocean before setting out on their long trip. Their flesh is imbued with rich flavour and becomes firm, succulent and plump – the long swim develops the muscles and flesh to produce a powerful, rippling body. After spawning, most of the salmon die, but some survive and go back to the sea to return to the river another year. The oldest recorded salmon had reached the grand old age of 13 years and had spawned four times before finally being caught on Loch Maree in Wester Ross.

The rise and fall of the salmon

Salmon was once so plentiful that it was despised by the upper classes. As a cheap, everyday filler, salmon was eaten fresh, dried, smoked and pickled. Tweed kettle – salmon gently simmered in white wine with shallots, herbs and mushrooms – was a very popular dish sold in Edinburgh cook shops in the 19th century, and could be said to be an early example of a takeaway meal.

Sadly, the wild salmon population is in decline, as overfishing and disease have gradually taken their toll. Fewer and fewer salmon are returning to the rivers to spawn. Salmon are especially vulnerable to pollution and clean oxygenated water is essential for them to spawn. The restricted waters of the few remaining salmon rivers remain unpolluted and so provide good breeding conditions.

Above *Atlantic salmon has deep pink flesh with a superb flavour.*

Wild salmon fishing

Fishing the rivers for wild salmon is now strictly controlled and you must purchase a licence for a specific part of a river beforehand. Keen anglers from around the world come to the Scottish Highlands throughout the year to enjoy fishing the traditional way and plenty of

Left *Salmon-fishing rivers are now highly restricted, especially during the spawning season.*

Above *Hand-sliced high-quality smoked salmon has become a speciality on the Islands.*

excellent food too. The River Tweed is one of the best salmon rivers in Europe, with a long season and a good supply of excellent salmon.

Salmon farming

Since the late 1960s, salmon farms have sprung up throughout the Highlands and Islands, many of them owned and run by Scandinavians who developed the technique throughout the previous decades. Farmed salmon has the advantage of being available all year round, and it is plentiful and cheaper than the wild version. It can now be found in every major store and supermarket around Scotland.

Much controversy rages over the subject of salmon farming. Critics say that the flavour and texture of farmed salmon is much inferior to that of the wild fish, and it is true that the taste of wild salmon is completely different from that of farmed. Farmed salmon also has a softer, slightly flabbier texture than its wild relative, perhaps because of its relatively easy life, being fed, spawned and reared in carefully controlled conditions.

Farming also causes environmental problems as it pollutes the lochs and coastal areas. Some producers have taken measures to ensure that their farms are environmentally friendly, and often organic too. A few high-quality farms have been developed to address both the environmental problems and to enhance the taste of the fish.

Smoked salmon

A flavoursome luxury, Scottish smoked salmon has become well known throughout the world for its quality and excellent taste. Many producers make speciality high-quality smoked salmon, smoked in aromatic woods for fine flavours and a delicately textured fish.

Curing and smoking salmon are skills which take years to master and which are performed by dedicated craftsmen and women. The flavour and colour of the smoked salmon will vary according to the cure, the type of fuel used and the type of smoking. The art is to blend these three elements well. The traditional process is to skin and fillet the fish first, then rest it in salt, before washing off the salt and placing the fish in a smoking oven for up to 48 hours. The fish is then thinly sliced by hand.

Smoked salmon makes its mark as a first course, traditionally served with wholemeal bread, lemon juice and ground black pepper. Recently it has become a popular appetizer, served on drop scones or Scotch pancakes with cream cheese or yogurt. The Scottish breakfast menu would not be complete without scrambled eggs and smoked salmon, and it is also used in main courses to add flavour to fish dishes.

Below *Salmon is traditionally smoked in large ovens lined with sliding shelves.*

Feasts and festivals

Festivities, celebrations and parties are key to Scottish culture. There are the raucous Scottish reels accompanied by Gaelic music played on the accordion, bagpipes and fiddle. There are Highland Games, Burns Night and Hogmanay. Perhaps the best-known events in Scotland are the Edinburgh International Festival and the Edinburgh Festival Fringe, which together showcase music, theatre and dance.

Below *Fireworks light the Edinburgh streets at midnight at the Hogmanay New Year's Eve festivities.*

Hogmanay

New Year's Eve in Scotland is Hogmanay. Festivities involve street parties, fireworks and costumes, especially in Edinburgh where the city centre is closed to normal traffic for the duration. The origins of the word Hogmanay are unknown. It may derive from the Norse *Hoggunott* or night of slaughter when animals were killed for a midwinter feast, or from *aguillanneuf*, the old French street cry for gifts on the eve of New Year. The traditional New Year song is "Auld Lang Syne"; the version sung today was reworked and made popular by Robert Burns, the famous Scottish poet.

A great many traditions surround Hogmanay, many related to food. The "first foot" in the house after midnight must be a dark-haired male, carrying symbolic coal, black bun or shortbread. Black bun is a very rich, dark fruitcake encased in pastry, usually accompanied by a wee dram. Clootie dumpling (clootie is the cloth in which the pudding is boiled) is a fruit pudding with a coin concealed inside. Traditionally, the person who got the coin was given the newborn lambs in the spring.

In Edinburgh and other parts of Scotland the traditional Hogmanay beverage until well into the 19th century was *het pint*, a potent blend of hot spiced ale, eggs and whisky. A couple of hours before midnight, great gleaming copper kettles of *het pint* were carried through the streets. Cupbearers pressed everyone into having a "noggin".

In Kirkwall, Orkney, a New Year Ba' Game takes place in the street on 1 January. Much merriment and excitement accompanies the game where the Uppies and the Doonies fight for a cork-filled leather ball.

Burns Night

Scottish communities throughout the world commemorate the birth, on 25 January 1759, of the poet Robert Burns with the traditional Burns Supper. The intimate and magical night is heavily ritualized. Before the meal begins Burns' Selkirk Grace is recited:

Some hae meat and canna eat
And some wad eat, that want it,
But we hae meat, and we can eat,
Sae let the Lord be thankit.

A piper enters, followed by the chef carrying the haggis. A waiter follows

Above A chef and piper bring in the haggis at a Burns Night supper.

behind carrying a bottle of whisky. They walk around the guests, ending at the top table, where the chairman takes the whisky and pours out two large glasses. The haggis is put on the table and the whiskies are given to the piper and to the chef. Then the haggis is "addressed" with the Burns poem "Address to a Haggis" (1786), which begins:

> *Fair fa' your honest, sonsie face,*
> *Great chieftain o' the puddin'-race!*

A dirk (dagger) is plunged into the haggis and a St Andrew's cross is cut on the top. It is served with bashed neeps and champit tatties – mashed turnips and creamed potatoes. After the meal is over there are whisky toasts to "The Immortal Memory" of Burns. The evening continues with Burns songs and ends with "Auld Lang Syne" and three cheers for absent friends.

The Edinburgh Festival

The plethora of cultural activities held over six weeks each year in the summer are collectively known as the Edinburgh International Festival. The largest arts festival in the world, the Edinburgh Festival has a splendid programme of events that includes art exhibitions, café concerts, talks, lectures and workshops plus live performances by internationally renowned artists. It attracts thousands of visitors from all over the world.

Food and drink are an essential part of the festival with farmers' markets offering local foods, lively food debates with top Scottish food writers and chefs, food-themed films, opportunities to sample beers from Scottish breweries, plus wine tastings from Scottish wine merchants and a chance to discover the origins of whisky with a wee dram or two on offer! There is plenty to eat and drink too as Edinburgh's finest cafés and restaurants offer a wide choice of food and drinks.

The Highland Games

Bursting with clan rivalry, the Highland Games have their roots in ancient Celtic traditions and originated with the clan meetings organized by the chiefs. The most important games are the Edinburgh Highland Games in August, and in September the Braemar Gathering and Highland Games, and the Aberdeen and Aboyne Highland Games.

Formalization and annual gatherings began around 1820 as part of the revival of tartan and Highland culture and in 1848 the Braemar Gathering was attended by Queen Victoria. The competitions were much as they are today, with traditional stone and

Below The Edinburgh streets are crowded with performers, stalls and food fairs during the Festival.

Right The Highland Games include a traditional dance competition with brightly coloured tartans.

hammer throwing, tossing the caber, piping and dancing, along with running and jumping events.

Food and whisky are abundant, with plenty of spit roasts and local pies. Raspberries and strawberries abound, served with fresh cream and shortbreads.

Harvest celebrations

In the Celtic year, *Lammas* heralded the start of the harvest and it was an annual fair day in most parts of Scotland until the 20th century. The gathering-in of a successful *hairst* (harvest) has been celebrated since ancient times, and the climax was the harvest feast or *kirn*, also known as the *muckle supper* (big supper).

Ale-crowdie (also called meal-and-ale) always featured at the harvest feast in Aberdeen and north-east Scotland, so much so that it gave its name to the festival. It was always made with the first of the grain, to commemorate the renewal of the food supply. The meal

was put in a large bowl or small wooden tub and ale was poured over until it was of drinking consistency – if it was too thin it was an omen that next year's crops would be poor. The drink was sweetened with treacle, laced with whisky and left to stand. Charms were concealed in the bowl and everyone present took a spoonful.

In the Highlands the new grain was made into a bannock known as *moilean moire*. In Orkney a fruited bannock was given as a reward to the man who carried the last load of sheaves into the stack yard. He was then given a head start and chased by the other men and only allowed to eat it when he had out-distanced his pursuers.

Cranachan or cream crowdie (from the Gaelic *cruaidh*, meaning thick and firm), a luscious combination of toasted oatmeal, cream, honey and whisky, was also essential at harvest celebrations.

Hallowe'en

The coming of Christianity replaced the old pagan feasts with religious festivals. Samhain or Samhuinn, the most important Celtic festival marking the start of winter, became the Eve of All Hallows (the night before All Saints' Day) or Hallowe'en on 31 October. It was a mysterious time when it was

Left Traditional Scottish music is played at many celebrations, with fiddles, guitars and accordians.

Above *Evening celebrations often involve a ceilidh with Scottish reeling.*

believed that ghosts, fairies, demons and witches wandered the earth. Bonfires were lit to ward off evil spirits, masks were worn to avoid being recognized by the spirits, and lucky charms protected against evil. Hallowe'en "guizing" and the wearing of masks and costumes is a remnant of those beliefs.

Hollowed-out turnips with a candle inside were placed on gateposts to frighten evil spirits – the origin of pumpkin lanterns today. The custom of eating special cakes probably derives from the practice of baking spiced cakes to herald the winter. Gingerbreads and biscuits were especially popular in Scotland.

Fortune-telling and magic were other traditional customs of Hallowe'en. A fortune-telling pudding (usually a large bowl of cranachan) contained small charms. Each charm had a specific meaning: a coin meant wealth, a ring foretold marriage and a thimble indicated no marriage.

Yule and Christmas festivities

Christmas festivities were banned by the Church in 1649 at the Reformation. The annual holiday was abolished and church ministers checked on their parishioners to make sure no festive foods or celebrations were in evidence. Proper festivities did not resume until the mid-18th century, and still today the New Year is the more important holiday of the midwinter period in Scotland.

Whipkull or *whipcol*, a mixture of beaten egg yolks and sugar, was served in a special bowl to the Shetland *Udallers* (lairds) at the great Yule breakfasts. Sometimes cream was added and later still a good measure of rum or whisky. Rich, crisp shortbread is the traditional accompaniment.

Atholl brose is another popular Christmas drink enjoyed on the days running up to Christmas Day. It is made from whisky, strained honey, oatmeal and sweet cream slowly beaten together in the right order and proportion. Its creation is credited to the Duke of Atholl when, during a Highland Rebellion in 1745, he foiled his enemy by filling the well from which they drank with the heady mixture. The intoxicated men were then easily defeated and the drink became more widely known.

Up-Helly-Aa

Torches, fireworks and bonfires light the night sky in this midwinter fire festival in Lerwick on Shetland. It is rooted in an ancient Viking festival, marking the end of Yule, and the 5,000 onlookers and participants dress as Vikings.

A full-sized replica of a Viking longboat is paraded through Lerwick by the Chief Guizer, who represents Sigurd Hlodvisson – Sigurd the Stout, Earl of Orkney, who died in 1014 on the battlefield at Clontarf, Ireland. In the early evening 850 torches are lit. The guizers throw them into the ship to set it ablaze. As they do so they sing "Up-Helly-Aa". Rockets and guns are fired from ships, and the longboat burns spectacularly. Fortified with whisky, the crowds sing the anthem, "The Norseman's Home".

Below *The midwinter fire festival of Up-Helly-Aa includes the burning of a Viking longboat.*

Quality foods for the future

Scottish foods have become celebrated around the world, from the excellent smoked salmon and other smoked goods to the highly prized beef and meats. Many classic Scottish recipes have survived virtually unchanged through the centuries, and their history offers a fascinating glimpse of the past. However, Scotland's food and cooking is not content to rest on its laurels, but continues to evolve and develop thanks to dedicated artisan food and drink producers, manufacturers and innovative chefs who skilfully incorporate new ingredients, along with modern ideas and cooking methods.

One of the main catalysts for change has been the explosion in tourism that has taken place in Scotland throughout the last few decades. Thousands flock to see the spectacular scenery and to enjoy the walking, hiking, skiing and other outdoor activities, such as sailing, white-water rafting and golf.

Below Scotland's cuisine has been transformed into a celebration of the natural flavours of fresh local produce.

To meet the new demand of discriminating tourists, cafés, restaurants and hotels around the country have transformed everyday fare into internationally acclaimed cuisine. Much of the food is based on traditional Scottish, but with a twist. It may be fused and blended with modern and global preparations, cooking and serving techniques, for example haggis prepared with apples in a puff pastry pie and served with a jus of local berries. Many chefs create their own versions of Scottish specialities, such as the popular variations on the "fish supper" theme.

The new tourism has attracted top chefs to the country, including many Scottish chefs returning from training abroad. Restaurants are rated by the quality of their cuisine and compete with each other to raise standards.

Scotland is now considered a luxury holiday destination, with excellent eating opportunities. Europe's first six-star hotel is to be created in a Highland castle over the coming years, paving the way for further excellence.

Above Mussels are grown on ropes at an organic farm on Loch Fyne for a reliable and good-quality harvest.

Fish and shellfish

There has been a huge growth in the quantity and quality of fish and shellfish products. This range of excellent foods on ready supply has been recognized as a quintessentially Scottish speciality and a plethora of traditional and modern producers have risen to the challenge.

The product ranges have become more diverse and include all sorts of smoked and prepared fish and shellfish, including new smoking flavours to produce delicate smoked salmon. The quality has increased enormously and advanced techniques, skills and a competitive market have resulted in superb fish and seafood.

The amount that is produced has also grown through the surge in new farming methods. Although some farms produce superb foods, watch out for some poor-quality farmed fish that can lack flavour and texture. Organic and environmentally considerate farms, such as the one at Loch Fyne, offer excellent fish and shellfish without harming the lochs and coastlines.

Above A fair and food market at the head of Loch Fyne celebrates the boom in new foods throughout Scotland.

Quality products for export

The Scottish food and drink export market has been growing rapidly over the last few decades. These exports are not only from large-scale producers but from smaller enterprises, often family-run, using local specialist ingredients.

Appreciation of the quality and refinement of Scotch whisky has spread around the globe. It is now one of the UK's top five exports and is exported to about 200 different markets.

Traditional dishes such as smoked salmon, shortbread and haggis have achieved international renown and high-quality products are exported for those living abroad. Several tons of haggis are exported for Burns Night suppers on 25 January. Haggis is very popular in France where it is now served in top Parisian restaurants. Shortbread, Scotland's national biscuit, is also much in demand and is exported all over the world. Baxters of Speyside export their delicious traditionally made marmalades, including the ever-popular Malt Whisky Marmalade.

New foods, new markets

Modern food enterprises have also proved successful – deer farming, the seaweed-fed sheep of the Shetlands, ice creams from the Orkney Isles and a host of new cheeses. There has also been a revival of ancient recipes, such as fruit and flower wines from Orkney, silver birch wine, heather ale, and spruce and pine ales from Viking days, making excellent gifts and souvenirs.

In every city, town and village throughout Scotland, you'll find both traditional and modern examples of Scottish products. The Bridge of Allan, a tiny village near Stirling, boasts one of the best food shops in Scotland, selling top-quality Scottish food and drink from both small specialist producers and larger manufacturers.

New markets continue to open up – organic foods, such as organic heather-fed lamb, are now popular. A new generation of chefs has devised imaginative and exciting ways to use Scottish produce to create modern recipes. Pubs and restaurants offer a wealth of different cuisines using local produce.

This is an exciting time for Scottish food and drink. Thanks to the efforts of the producers who constantly strive to ensure that it is recognized as the best in the world, it looks likely that the future of Scottish food is assured for generations to come.

Below Specialist cheeses are made for local dishes and for export, such as these from the Sgriob-Ruadh Dairy near Tobermory on the Isle of Mull.

Breakfasts

A good hearty Scottish breakfast is the ideal
way to start the morning, especially if your day
involves energetic outdoor activities. Oats take
many forms, from porridge to oatcakes, and
smoked fish, such as smoked haddock and
salmon, is also popular. The national favourite,
black pudding, is a traditional breakfast
staple, often served with eggs, bacon and
rowies, a special breakfast roll enjoyed with
jam or marmalade.

Porridge

One of Scotland's oldest foods, oatmeal porridge remains a favourite way to start the day, especially during winter. Brown sugar or honey, cream and a tot of whisky are treats added for weekend breakfasts and to spoil guests in some of the best guesthouses and hotels.

Serves 4

1 litre/1¾ pints/4 cups water

115g/4oz/1 cup pinhead oatmeal

good pinch of salt

Variation Modern rolled oats can be used, in the proportion of 115g/4oz/ generous 1 cup to 750ml/1¼ pints/3 cups water, plus a sprinkling of salt. This cooks more quickly than pinhead oatmeal. Simmer, stirring to prevent sticking, for about 5 minutes. Either type of oatmeal can be left to cook overnight in the slow oven of a range.

1 Put the water, pinhead oatmeal and salt into a heavy pan and bring to the boil over a medium heat, stirring with a wooden spatula. When the porridge is smooth and beginning to thicken, reduce the heat to a simmer.

2 Cook gently for about 25 minutes, stirring occasionally, until the oatmeal is cooked and the consistency smooth. Serve hot with cold milk and extra salt, if required. It is frequently served with chopped fresh fruit.

Per portion Energy 115kcal/488kJ; Protein 3.6g; Carbohydrate 20.9g, of which sugars 0g; Fat 2.5g, of which saturates 0g; Cholesterol 0mg; Calcium 16mg; Fibre 2g; Sodium 304mg.

Potato cakes

This is the traditional method of making potato cakes on a griddle or in a heavy frying pan. Commercial versions are available throughout Scotland as thin, pre-cooked potato cakes, which are fried to eat with a full breakfast or to enjoy at high tea.

Makes about 12

675g/1½lb potatoes, peeled

25g/1oz/2 tbsp unsalted (sweet) butter

about 175g/6oz/1½ cups plain (all-purpose) flour

salt

1 Boil the potatoes in a large pan over a medium heat until tender, then drain thoroughly, replacing the pan with the drained poatoes over a low heat for a few minutes to allow any moisture to evaporate completely.

2 Mash the potatoes with plenty of salt, then mix in the butter and cool.

3 Turn out on to a floured work surface and knead in about one-third of its volume in flour, or as much as is needed to make a pliable dough.

4 Roll out to a thickness of about 1cm/½in and cut into triangles.

5 Heat a dry griddle or heavy frying pan over a low heat and cook the potato cakes on it for about 3 minutes on each side until browned. Serve hot.

Per batch Energy 1276kcal/5392kJ; Protein 30.4g; Carbohydrate 249.1g, of which sugars 6.7g; Fat 24.1g, of which saturates 13.4g; Cholesterol 53mg; Calcium 282mg; Fibre 14g; Sodium 203mg.

Rowies

These are the delicious traditional breakfast rolls served in Scottish homes, originally coming from Aberdeenshire, although they are made all over the country today and are very popular in tourist areas. They are eaten like a croissant, hot from the oven with butter or fresh cream and marmalades or jams and jellies.

Makes 16

7.5ml/1½ tsp dried yeast

15ml/1 tbsp soft light brown sugar

450ml/¾ pint/scant 2 cups warm water

450g/1lb/4 cups strong white bread flour

pinch of salt

225g/8oz/1 cup butter

115g/4oz/½ cup lard or white cooking fat

1 Mix the yeast with the sugar, dissolve in a little warm water taken from the measured amount then set aside in a warm place, lightly covered to allow some air to circulate.

2 Mix the flour in a large mixing bowl with the salt. When the yeast has bubbled up pour it into the flour with the rest of the water. Mix well to form a dough and leave in a warm place covered with a dish towel to rise until it has doubled in size, about 2 hours.

3 Cream the butter and lard or white cooking fat together in a small bowl and then divide the mixture into three portions. The mixture should be soft enough to spread easily but not warm enough to melt. If it is melting, refrigerate for 5–10 minutes.

4 When the dough has doubled in size, knock back (punch down) until it is the original size. Roll it out on a floured surface to a rectangle about 1cm/½in thick. Spread a third of the butter mixture over two-thirds of the dough.

5 Fold the ungreased third of the dough over on to the greased middle third, then the other greased third into the middle, thus giving three layers. Roll this back to the original rectangle size. Leave to rest in a cool place for 40 minutes then repeat the procedure, including the resting period, twice more, to use up the butter mixture.

6 Cut the dough into 16 squares. Shape into rough circles by folding the edges in all the way around and place on a baking sheet. Leave to rise, covered with a clean dry dish towel, for 45 minutes. Meanwhile preheat the oven to 200°C/400°F/Gas 6.

7 When the rowies have risen, bake in the oven for 15 minutes until golden brown and flaky.

Per portion Energy 296kcal/1233kJ; Protein 3g; Carbohydrate 25.4g, of which sugars 1.5g; Fat 21g, of which saturates 11.4g; Cholesterol 41mg; Calcium 47mg; Fibre 1g; Sodium 96mg.

Kedgeree

Of Indian origin, kedgeree came to Scotland via England and the landed gentry.
It quickly became a well-known dish using smoked fish for breakfast or high tea. This is
a more manageable dish than the full Scottish breakfast when feeding several people,
and it is often served in guesthouses and restaurants.

Serves 4–6

450g/1lb smoked haddock

300ml/½ pint/1¼ cups milk

175g/6oz/scant 1 cup long grain rice

pinch of grated nutmeg and
cayenne pepper

50g/2oz/¼ cup butter

1 onion, peeled and finely chopped

2 hard-boiled eggs

salt and ground black pepper

chopped fresh parsley, to garnish

lemon wedges and wholemeal
(whole-wheat) toast, to serve

1 Poach the haddock in the milk, made up with just enough water to cover the fish, for about 8 minutes, or until just cooked. Skin the haddock, remove all the bones and flake the flesh with a fork. Set aside.

2 Bring 600ml/1 pint/2½ cups water to the boil in a large pan. Add the rice, cover closely with a lid and cook over a low heat for about 25 minutes, or until all the water has been absorbed by the rice. Season with salt and a grinding of black pepper, and the nutmeg and cayenne pepper.

3 Meanwhile, heat 15g/½oz/1 tbsp butter in a pan and fry the onion until soft and transparent. Set aside. Roughly chop one of the hard-boiled eggs, and slice the other into neat wedges.

4 Stir the remaining butter into the rice and add the flaked haddock, onion and the chopped egg. Season to taste and heat the mixture through gently (this can be done on a serving dish in a low oven if more convenient).

5 To serve, pile up the kedgeree on a warmed dish, sprinkle generously with parsley and arrange the wedges of egg on top. Put the lemon wedges around the base and serve hot with the toast.

Variation Try using leftover cooked salmon, instead of the haddock.

Per portion Energy 399kcal/1668kJ; Protein 28.9g; Carbohydrate 38g, of which sugars 2.2g; Fat 14.6g, of which saturates 7.6g; Cholesterol 181mg; Calcium 62mg; Fibre 0.5g; Sodium 974mg.

Smoked haddock with spinach and poached egg

This is a really special breakfast treat. Use young spinach leaves in season and, of course, the freshest eggs. There is something about the combination of eggs, spinach and "smoke" that really perks you up in the morning.

Serves 4

4 undyed smoked haddock fillets

milk

75ml/2½fl oz/⅓ cup double (heavy) cream

25g/1oz/2 tbsp butter

250g/9oz fresh spinach, tough stalks removed

white wine vinegar

4 eggs

salt and ground black pepper

1 Over a low heat, poach the haddock fillets in just enough milk to come halfway up the fish, shaking the pan gently to keep the fish moist, for about 5 minutes. When cooked remove the fish and keep warm.

2 Increase the heat under the milk and allow to reduce by about half, stirring occasionally. Add the cream and allow to bubble up. Season to taste with salt and pepper. The sauce should be thickened but should pour easily.

3 Heat a frying pan then add the butter. Add the spinach, stirring briskly for a few minutes. Season lightly then set aside, keeping it warm.

4 To poach the eggs, bring 4cm/1½in water to a simmer and add a few drops of vinegar. Gently crack two eggs into the water and cook for 3 minutes. Remove the first egg using a slotted spoon and rest in the spoon on some kitchen paper to remove any water. Repeat with the second egg, then cook the other two in the same way.

5 Place the spinach over the fillets and a poached egg on top. Pour over the cream sauce and serve immediately.

Per portion Energy 350kcal/1455kJ; Protein 27.5g; Carbohydrate 1.5g, of which sugars 1.4g; Fat 26.3g, of which saturates 14g; Cholesterol 277mg; Calcium 170mg; Fibre 1.3g; Sodium 969mg.

Smoked haddock and cheese omelette

This creamy, smoked haddock soufflé omelette is a variation of Omelette Arnold Bennett, which was created at the Savoy Hotel for the famous author who frequently dined there. It is now served all over the world, using good Scottish smoked haddock and cheese.

Serves 2

175g/6oz smoked haddock fillet, poached and drained

50g/2oz/½ cup butter, diced

175ml/6fl oz/¾ cup whipping or double (heavy) cream

4 eggs, separated

40g/1½oz/⅓ cup mature (sharp) Cheddar cheese, grated

ground black pepper

watercress, to garnish

1 Remove the skin and any bones from the haddock fillet by carefully pressing down the length of each fillet with your fingertips. Discard them. Using a fork and following the grain of the flesh, flake the flesh into large chunks.

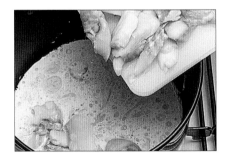

2 Melt half the butter with 60ml/4 tbsp of the cream in a fairly small non-stick pan. Wait until the mixture is hot but not boiling, and then add the chunks of flaked fish. Stir together gently, making sure that you do not break up the flakes of fish. Bring slowly to the boil, stirring continuously. Once it is boiling, cover the pan with a lid, remove from the heat and set aside to cool for at least 20 minutes.

3 Preheat the grill (broiler) to high. Mix the egg yolks with 15ml/1 tbsp of the cream. Season with ground black pepper, then stir into the fish. In a separate bowl, mix the cheese and the remaining cream. Stiffly whisk the egg whites, then fold into the fish mixture.

4 Heat the remaining butter in an omelette pan until it is slightly bubbling. Add the fish mixture and cook until it is browned underneath. Pour the cheese mixture over evenly and grill (broil) until it is bubbling.

5 Serve on a warmed plate immediately, garnished with watercress and with fresh crusty bread to accompany.

Cook's Tip
Try to buy smoked haddock that does not contain artificial colouring for this recipe. Besides being better for you, it gives the omelette a lighter, more attractive colour.

Per portion Energy 821kcal/3396kJ; Protein 36.1g; Carbohydrate 2.6g, of which sugars 2.6g; Fat 74g, of which saturates 42.6g; Cholesterol 577mg; Calcium 280mg; Fibre 0g; Sodium 1123mg.

Smoked haddock and bacon

This is a classic combination, very much associated with Scotland. The smokiness of the fish goes well with the rich flavour of the bacon – both are complemented by the creamy sauce.

Serves 4

25g/1oz/2 tbsp butter

4 undyed smoked haddock fillets

8 rashers (strips) lean back bacon

120ml/4floz/½ cup double (heavy) cream

ground black pepper

chopped fresh chives, to garnish

1 Preheat the grill (broiler) to medium. Over a gentle heat, melt the butter in a frying pan.

2 Add the haddock fillets, working in two batches if necessary, and cook gently, turning once, for about 3 minutes each side. When cooked, place in a large ovenproof dish and cover. Reserve the juices from the frying pan.

3 Grill (broil) the bacon, turning once, until just cooked through but not crispy. Leave the grill on.

4 Return the frying pan to the heat and pour in the cream and any reserved juices from the haddock. Bring to the boil then simmer briefly, stirring occasionally. Season to taste with ground black pepper.

5 Meanwhile place two bacon rashers over each haddock fillet and place the dish under the grill (broiler) briefly. Then pour over the hot creamy sauce, garnish with snipped fresh chives and serve immediately.

Variation
Instead of topping the smoked haddock with bacon, use wilted spinach for a healthier, tasty option. Thoroughly wash a good handful of spinach for each person. Then plunge it into boiling water for 3 minutes, drain well and lay across each fillet.

Per portion Energy 391kcal/1624kJ; Protein 28.8g; Carbohydrate 0.5g, of which sugars 0.5g; Fat 30.5g, of which saturates 16.5g; Cholesterol 119mg; Calcium 40mg; Fibre 0g; Sodium 1671mg.

Creamy scrambled eggs with smoked salmon

A special treat for weekend breakfasts, eggs served this way are popular in some of Scotland's best guesthouses and hotels and are a good alternative to the traditional fry-up.

Serves 1

3 eggs

15ml/1 tbsp single (light) cream or milk

knob (pat) of butter

1 slice of smoked salmon, chopped or whole, warmed

salt and ground black pepper

sprig of fresh parsley, to garnish

triangles of hot toast, to serve

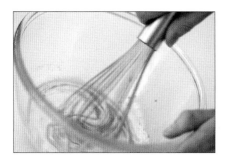

1 Whisk the eggs in a bowl together with half the cream or milk, a generous grinding of black pepper and a little salt to taste if you like, remembering that the smoked salmon may be quite naturally salty.

2 Melt the butter in a pan then add the egg mixture and stir until nearly set. Add the rest of the cream, which prevents the eggs from overcooking.

3 Either stir in the chopped smoked salmon or serve the warmed slice alongside the egg. Serve immediately on warmed plates.

Variation
For creamy scrambled eggs with bacon and cheese, first cook 1 or 2 rashers (strips) of streaky (fatty) bacon per person in a non-stick frying pan until crispy. Then chop the bacon, add it to the egg mixture and scramble over a gentle heat as above. Just before it sets, add 25g/1oz/¼ cup grated hard cheese, such as Cheddar, and some freshly chopped herbs of your choice – basil or chives work well. Mix together quickly and serve immediately on hot buttered toast or freshly baked bread.

Per portion Energy 447kcal/1862kJ; Protein 37.3g; Carbohydrate 0.4g, of which sugars 0.4g; Fat 33.6g, of which saturates 13.1g; Cholesterol 734mg; Calcium 128mg; Fibre 0g; Sodium 1.37g.

Black pudding with potato and apple

This traditional blood sausage has come a long way from its once humble position in Scottish cooking. Made throughout Scotland and widely available, black pudding is now extremely popular, and even features on many a contemporary restaurant menu.

Serves 4

4 large potatoes, peeled

45ml/3 tbsp olive oil

8 slices of black pudding (blood sausage), such as Clonakilty

115g/4oz cultivated mushrooms, such as oyster or shiitake

2 eating apples, peeled, cored and cut into wedges

25ml/1½ tbsp sherry vinegar or wine vinegar

15g/½oz/1 tbsp butter

salt and ground black pepper

1 Grate the potatoes, putting them into a bowl of water as you grate them. Drain and squeeze out any moisture.

2 Heat 30ml/2 tbsp of the olive oil in a large non-stick frying pan, add the grated potatoes and season. Press the potatoes into the pan with your hands.

3 Cook the potatoes until browned, then turn over and cook the other side. When cooked, slide on to a warmed plate.

4 Heat the remaining oil and sauté the black pudding and mushrooms together for a few minutes. Remove from the pan and keep warm.

5 Add the apple wedges to the frying pan and gently sauté to colour them golden brown. Add the sherry or wine vinegar to the apples, and boil up the juices. Add the butter, stir with a wooden spatula until it has melted and season to taste with salt and ground black pepper.

6 Cut the potato cake into portion-sized wedges and divide among four warmed plates. Arrange the slices of black pudding and cooked mushrooms on the bed of potato cake, pour over the apples and the warm juices and serve immediately.

Per portion Energy 247kcal/1034kJ; Protein 4.2g; Carbohydrate 28.8g, of which sugars 5.4g; Fat 13.6g, of which saturates 4g; Cholesterol 13mg; Calcium 16mg; Fibre 2.4g; Sodium 132mg.

Laver bread and bacon omelette

Laver bread is a tasty seaweed preparation perhaps more commonly associated with the Welsh, but it has been used in Scotland for centuries. Dried or canned versions are available and avoid the long preparation time, but if you prefer, use boiled spinach instead.

Makes 1 omelette

oil, to prepare the pan

3 eggs

10ml/2 tsp butter

1 rasher (strip) lean back bacon, cooked and diced

25g/1oz prepared laver bread

salt and ground black pepper

1 Heat a little oil in an omelette pan then leave for a few minutes to help season the pan. A non-stick or small curved-sided pan may also be used.

2 Break the eggs into a bowl large enough for whisking, season then whisk until the yolk and white are well combined but not frothy.

3 Pour the oil out of the pan and reheat. Add the butter, which should begin to sizzle straight away. If it does not the pan is too cool or if it burns it is too hot. Rinse out, dry and try again.

4 Pour the whisked eggs into the pan and immediately, using the back of a fork, draw the mixture towards the middle of the pan, working from the outside and using quick circular movements going around the pan.

5 As it is beginning to cook but is not quite set, put the bacon and laver bread evenly over one half of the omelette. Cook for another 30 seconds then remove from the heat.

6 Fold one side of the mixture over the side with the bacon and laver bread, leave for a minute or two, then turn out on to a warmed plate. Serve immediately while piping hot.

Per portion Energy 355kcal/1472kJ; Protein 23.6g; Carbohydrate 0.5g, of which sugars 0.4g; Fat 29.2g, of which saturates 11.4g; Cholesterol 605mg; Calcium 131mg; Fibre 0.5g; Sodium 691mg.

Lamb's kidneys with a devil sauce

This is one of those hearty dishes that the Scots are so good at, ideal as a breakfast dish, served with rice, for when you are about to go out for a day's walking or stalking game on the hills and highlands. It can also be accompanied with creamy mashed potato for an enjoyable yet easy-to-prepare lunch or supper.

Serves 4

12 lamb's kidneys

45ml/3 tbsp vegetable oil

15ml/1 tbsp Worcestershire sauce

15ml/1 tbsp Mushroom Sauce

pinch of cayenne pepper

175g/6oz/¾ cup butter

10ml/2 tsp English (hot) mustard

10ml/2 tsp French mustard

1 Skin the kidneys and slice them in half horizontally. Push the flesh out of the way with a finger to reveal all the white gristle. Use a sharp-pointed pair of scissors or a very sharp vegetable knife to remove the central gristly core and any fat.

Variation
These kidneys make an excellent savoury for serving at the end of a formal dinner. Spoon small portions on to rounds of fried bread. You will only need one whole kidney per person.

2 Heat the oil in a frying pan and cook the kidneys over a high heat for a few minutes on both sides, leaving them a little pink. Pour off any excess fat from the pan and set aside to allow the kidneys to cool a little.

3 Meanwhile mix together all the other ingredients in a bowl, using the back of the spoon to break up the sauces.

4 Spread the mixture over the kidneys and return to the heat. Cook gently until the butter melts, then serve.

Per portion Energy 542kcal/2246kJ; Protein 26g; Carbohydrate 1.1g, of which sugars 1g; Fat 48.3g, of which saturates 25.1g; Cholesterol 566mg; Calcium 29mg; Fibre 0g; Sodium 609mg.

Lorn sausage with red onion relish

The Firth of Lorn, the region from which this dish originated, cuts through Argyll between the island of Mull and the mainland on the west coast of Scotland. Prepared simply and traditionally in a loaf shape and chilled overnight, the sausage is then sliced before cooking. Accompanied by cranberry and red onion relish, it makes a delicious meal.

Serves 4

900g/2lb minced (ground) beef

65g/2½oz/generous 1 cup stale white breadcrumbs

150g/5oz/scant 1 cup semolina

5ml/1 tsp salt

75ml/5 tbsp water

ground black pepper

Cranberry and Red Onion Relish, to serve

1 In a large mixing bowl, combine the beef, breadcrumbs, semolina and salt together thoroughly with a fork. Pour in the water, mix again and season to taste. Pass the beef mixture through a coarse mincer (grinder) and set aside.

2 Carefully line a 1.3kg/3lb loaf tin (pan) with clear film (plastic wrap).

3 Spoon the sausage mixture into the tin, pressing it in firmly with the back of a wooden spoon. Even out the surface and fold the clear film over the top. Chill overnight.

4 When ready to cook, preheat the grill (broiler). Turn the sausage out of the tin on to a chopping board and cut into 1cm/½in slices. Grill (broil) each slice until cooked through, turning once. Alternatively, fry until cooked through, again turning once.

Cook's Tip

For the best results, use standard minced (ground) beef for these sausages rather than lean minced steak, as the higher fat content is needed to bind the ingredients together.

Per portion Energy 691kcal/2886kJ; Protein 50.1g; Carbohydrate 40.7g, of which sugars 0.4g; Fat 37.4g, of which saturates 15.6g; Cholesterol 135mg; Calcium 47mg; Fibre 1.1g; Sodium 299mg.

Soups and appetizers

Tasty vegetable soups, refreshing, light salads,
and shellfish from Scotland's extensive coastline,
locks and rivers can make the perfect first
course to any meal. In this chapter there are
many traditional dishes to enjoy, from a
warming Scotch Broth and an aromatic
Cabbage and Potato Soup with Caraway to a
flavoursome Watercress Salad with Pear and
Dunsyre Blue Dressing or the impressive
Hot Crab Soufflés.

Cabbage and potato soup with caraway

Earthy floury potatoes are essential to the success of this soup, so choose your variety carefully. Caraway seeds come from a plant in the parsley family. They are aromatic and nutty, with a delicate anise flavour, adding a subtle accent to this satisfying dish.

Serves 4

30ml/2 tbsp olive oil

2 small onions, sliced

6 garlic cloves, halved

350g/12oz/3 cups shredded green cabbage

4 potatoes, unpeeled

5ml/1 tsp caraway seeds

5ml/1 tsp sea salt

1.2 litres/2 pints/5 cups water

1 Pour the olive oil into a large pan and soften the onion. Add the garlic and the cabbage and cook over a low heat for 10 minutes, stirring occasionally to prevent the cabbage from sticking.

2 Add the potatoes, caraway seeds, sea salt and water. Bring to the boil then simmer until all the vegetables are cooked through, about 20–30 minutes.

3 Remove from the heat and allow to cool slightly before mashing into a purée or passing through a sieve.

Cook's Tip
Use floury potatoes to achieve the correct texture for this soup. King Edward or Maris Piper (US russet or Idaho) are excellent choices.

Per portion Energy 144Kcal/601kJ; Protein 3.1g; Carbohydrate 20.4g, of which sugars 8.1g; Fat 6g, of which saturates 0.9g; Cholesterol 0mg; Calcium 60mg; Fibre 3.3g; Sodium 507mg.

Avocado, spinach and sorrel soup

Sorrel, with its sharp lemony flavour, grows wild throughout the UK, Europe, North America and Asia. In some parts of Scotland it is known as "sourocks", a reference to its sharp or sour flavour. It is delicious in salads and soups.

Serves 4

30ml/2 tbsp olive oil

2 onions, chopped

1kg/2¼lb spinach

900ml/1½ pints/3¾ cups light chicken stock

4 garlic cloves, crushed with salt

1 bunch sorrel leaves

2 avocados, peeled and stoned (pitted)

1 Pour the olive oil into a large heavy pan and sweat the onions over a gentle heat until soft but not coloured. Meanwhile, wash the spinach thoroughly and remove the stalks.

2 Add the spinach to the onions and cook for about 2 minutes, stirring, to wilt the leaves. Cover and increase the heat slightly then cook for a further 3 minutes. Add the stock, cover again and simmer for about 10 minutes.

3 Add the garlic, sorrel and avocados to the soup and once heated through remove from the heat.

4 Allow the soup to cool then purée in a blender. Reheat the soup before serving with warmed crusty bread.

Cook's Tips

• Crushing garlic in salt helps to bring out the oils of the garlic and also stops any being wasted in a garlic press. Use a coarse salt and try to keep a chopping board or at least a corner of one for this sole purpose, as it is hard to get rid of the scent of garlic and it can taint other foods.

• When using avocados in soup do not let them boil as this makes them taste bitter. They are best added at the end and just heated through.

• This soup freezes for up to a month. Freeze it the day you make it.

Per portion Energy 282kcal/1161kJ; Protein 9.3g; Carbohydrate 11.4g, of which sugars 8.3g; Fat 22.1g, of which saturates 4.1g; Cholesterol 0mg; Calcium 452mg; Fibre 8.9g; Sodium 357mg.

Mussel and fennel bree

Bree is the Scots word for a soup or broth, most often associated with shellfish rather like a bisque or bouillabaisse. Mussels partner particularly well with the anise flavour of Pernod or Ricard. Try to get the native Scottish mussels that are smaller with a good flavour.

Serves 4

1kg/2¼lb fresh mussels

1 fennel bulb

120ml/4fl oz/½ cup dry white wine

1 leek, finely sliced

olive oil

25g/1oz/2 tbsp butter

splash of Pernod or Ricard

150ml/¼ pint/⅔ cup double (heavy) cream

25g/1oz fresh parsley, chopped

1 Clean the mussels thoroughly, removing any beards and scraping off any barnacles. Discard any that are broken or open.

2 Strip off the outer leaves of the fennel and roughly chop them. Set to one side. Then take the central core of the fennel and chop it very finely. Set it aside in a separate dish or bowl.

3 Place the roughly chopped fennel leaves, the mussels and the wine in a large pan, cover and cook gently until all the mussels open, about 5 minutes. Discard any that remain closed.

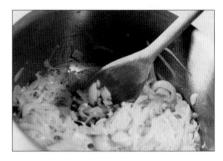

4 In a second pan sweat the leek and finely chopped core of the fennel gently in the oil and butter until soft.

5 Meanwhile remove the mussels from the first pan and either leave in the shell or remove. Set aside.

6 Strain the liquor on to the leek mixture and bring to the boil. Add a little water and the pastis, and simmer for a few minutes. Add the cream and parsley and bring back to the boil.

7 Place the mussels in a serving tureen and pour over the soup. Serve with crusty bread for mopping up the juices.

Cook's Tip
Farmed or "rope-grown" mussels are easier to clean. If you use mussels with lots of barnacles you will need to remove these first.

Per portion Energy 392kcal/1624kJ; Protein 13.4g; Carbohydrate 5.7g, of which sugars 3g; Fat 33g, of which saturates 16.9g; Cholesterol 105mg; Calcium 95mg; Fibre 2.8g; Sodium 297mg.

Scotch broth

Sustaining and warming, Scotch broth is custom-made for the chilly Scottish weather, and makes a delicious winter soup anywhere. Traditionally, a large pot of it is made and this is dipped into throughout the next few days, the flavour improving all the time.

Serves 6–8

1kg/2¼lb lean neck (US shoulder or breast) of lamb, cut into large, even-sized chunks

1.75 litres/3 pints/7½ cups cold water

1 large onion, chopped

50g/2oz/¼ cup pearl barley

bouquet garni

1 large carrot, chopped

1 turnip, chopped

3 leeks, chopped

1 small white cabbage, finely shredded

salt and ground black pepper

chopped fresh parsley, to garnish

1 Put the lamb and water in a large pan over a medium heat and gently bring to the boil. Skim off the scum with a spoon. Add the onion, pearl barley and bouquet garni, and stir in thoroughly.

2 Bring the soup back to the boil, then reduce the heat, partly cover the pan and simmer gently for a further 1 hour. Make sure that it does not boil too furiously or go dry.

3 Add the remaining vegetables to the pan and season with salt and ground black pepper. Bring to the boil, partly cover again and simmer for about 35 minutes, until the vegetables are tender.

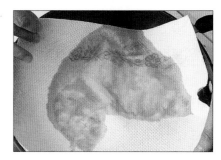

4 Remove the surplus fat from the top of the soup with a sheet of kitchen paper. Serve the soup hot, garnished with chopped parsley, with chunks of fresh bread.

Per portion Energy 387kcal/1619kJ; Protein 36.2g; Carbohydrate 17.7g, of which sugars 9.1g; Fat 19.5g, of which saturates 8.8g; Cholesterol 127mg; Calcium 86mg; Fibre 4.3g; Sodium 157mg.

Watercress salad with pear and Dunsyre Blue dressing

A refreshing light salad, this dish combines lovely peppery watercress, soft juicy pears and a tart dressing. Dunsyre is on the edge of the Pentland Hills in the Borders, and Dunsyre Blue has a wonderfully sharp flavour with a crumbly texture.

Serves 4

25g/1oz Dunsyre Blue cheese

30ml/2 tbsp walnut oil

15ml/1 tbsp lemon juice

2 bunches of watercress, thoroughly washed and trimmed

2 ripe pears (see Cook's Tips)

salt and ground black pepper

1 Crumble and then mash the Dunsyre Blue into the walnut oil.

2 Whisk in the lemon juice to create a thickish mixture. If you need to thicken it further, add a little more cheese. Season to taste with salt and ground black pepper.

3 Arrange a pile of watercress on the side of four plates.

4 Peel and slice the two pears then place the pear slices to the side of the watercress, allowing half a pear per person. You can also put the pear slices on top of the watercress, if you prefer. Drizzle the dressing over the salad.

Cook's Tips
• Choose Comice or similar pears that are soft and juicy for this salad.
• If you want to get things ready in advance, peel and slice the pears then rub with some lemon juice; this will stop them discolouring so quickly.

Per portion Energy 106kcal/442kJ; Protein 2.3g; Carbohydrate 7.6g, of which sugars 7.6g; Fat 7.6g, of which saturates 1.8g; Cholesterol 5mg; Calcium 81mg; Fibre 2g; Sodium 91mg.

Quail's egg salad with Bishop Kennedy cheese

Bishop Kennedy was originally made in the medieval monasteries of France, but now it is produced in Scotland. It is a full-fat soft cheese, with its rind washed in malt whisky to produce a distinctive orangey red crust and a strong creamy taste. It is runny when ripe.

Serves 4

8 quail's eggs

vinegar, for poaching

½ red onion, finely chopped

½ leek, cut into fine strips and blanched

75g/3oz Bishop Kennedy cheese, finely diced

½ red cabbage, shredded

mixed salad leaves, including Little Gem (Bibb) lettuce and lollo bionda

10ml/2 tsp pine nuts

salad dressing

1 Poach the quail's eggs. You need a shallow pan of simmering water with a dash of vinegar added, an eggcup, a slotted spoon, a pan of iced water. Using a thin knife, carefully break the shell of an egg and open it up into the eggcup. Gently lower the cup into the simmering water, allowing some water to cover and firm up the egg, then let it slide into the water and cook for about 2 minutes. The white should change from opaque to just white. Lift the egg out with a slotted spoon and put it straight into iced water.

2 When all the eggs are cooked lift them out of the water and dry them on kitchen paper. This last bit can be done just before you assemble the salad since the quail's eggs will keep in cold water for up to a couple of days.

3 Combine the salad ingredients, including the pine nuts (which can be lightly toasted if you like). Toss with your chosen dressing. To serve, simply place the diced Bishop Kennedy and the quail's eggs on top of the salad.

Per portion Energy 231kcal/956kJ; Protein 11.7g; Carbohydrate 5.3g, of which sugars 4.8g; Fat 17.7g, of which saturates 5.6g; Cholesterol 132mg; Calcium 203mg; Fibre 2.3g; Sodium 183mg.

Langoustines with saffron and tomato

The best langoustines come from the west coast of Scotland, where everything from a tiny shrimp to just smaller than a lobster is called a prawn. Langoustines, also known as Dublin Bay prawns or Norway lobsters, look like miniature lobsters, although they taste more like jumbo prawns or shrimp, and these can be substituted if you prefer.

Serves 4

5ml/1 tsp sea salt

20 live langoustines or Dublin Bay prawns (jumbo shrimp)

1 onion

15ml/1 tbsp olive oil

pinch of saffron threads

120ml/4fl oz/½ cup dry white wine

450g/1lb ripe fresh or canned tomatoes, roughly chopped

chopped fresh flat leaf parsley, to garnish

salt and ground black pepper

1 Bring a large pan of water to the boil, add the salt and plunge the shellfish into the pan. Let the water return to the boil then transfer the shellfish to a colander to cool.

Variation
You can also use other kinds of shellfish for this dish, such as mussels or clams. You will need to adjust the cooking times. Lobster also goes well in this recipe if you are serving a large number of people for a special occasion.

2 When cooled, shell the langoustines or prawns and reserve four heads with two claws each. Keep the rest of the shells, heads and claws to make a flavourful stock for the sauce.

3 Chop the onions. Heat a large heavy pan and add 15ml/1 tbsp olive oil. Gently fry the chopped onion to soften.

4 Stir in the saffron threads. Then add the shellfish debris, including the heads and the pincers. Stir to mix thoroughly and then reduce the heat.

5 Add the wine and then the tomatoes. Simmer to soften the tomatoes – this will take about 5 minutes. Do not allow the mixture to become too dry; add water if necessary.

6 Strain through a sieve, pushing the debris to get as much moisture out as possible. The resulting sauce should be light in texture; if it's too thick add some water. Check the seasoning.

7 Add the langoustines or prawns and warm over a gentle heat for a few minutes. Serve in warmed soup plates garnished with the reserved langoustine or prawn heads and scattered with chopped fresh flat leaf parsley.

Cook's Tip
Crushing the langoustine or prawn shell debris with a rolling pin before adding it to the pan helps to extract more flavour into the juices.

Per portion Energy 107kcal/449kJ; Protein 9.8g; Carbohydrate 4.9g, of which sugars 4.5g; Fat 3.4g, of which saturates 0.6g; Cholesterol 98mg; Calcium 54mg; Fibre 1.3g; Sodium 598mg.

Mussels with Musselburgh leeks

Musselburgh is a former fishing port near Edinburgh, famous for its oyster beds and its leeks – a short, stumpy variety with huge green tops and an excellent flavour. This recipe makes use of both the pale tender and dark green parts.

Serves 4

1.3kg/3lb mussels

1 leek, cut into 5cm/2in lengths

50g/2oz/¼ cup butter

1 onion, finely chopped

pinch of saffron threads

150ml/¼ pint/⅔ cup dry white wine

1 bay leaf

sprig of fresh thyme

6 black peppercorns

100ml/3½ fl oz/scant ½ cup double (heavy) cream

ground black pepper

chopped fresh parsley, to garnish

1 Scrub the mussels in plenty of cold water and discard any that are broken or remain open when tapped lightly. Remove the beard by pulling hard towards the pointed tip of the mussel. Use as small, sharp knife to scrape off any barnacles.

2 Thoroughly wash the leek, discard any tough outer leaves and cut into fine strips or batons.

3 Melt the butter in a heavy pan then sweat the onion gently until soft. Add the saffron threads and stir for a few minutes, then add the leek batons and allow to wilt slightly. Add the mussels with the wine, herbs and peppercorns. Cover and steam over a medium heat until the mussel shells open, about 5 minutes. Discard any that remain closed.

4 Remove the lid from the pan and add the cream. Simmer rapidly to allow the sauce to thicken slightly. Remove the bay leaf and thyme, and stir well to mix the leek around.

5 Serve immediately in warmed bowls, with a grind or two of black pepper and garnished with lots of chopped fresh parsley. Provide hot, crusty bread for mopping up the sauce.

Per portion Energy 332kcal/1379kJ; Protein 17.6g; Carbohydrate 1.9g, of which sugars 1.6g; Fat 25.7g, of which saturates 15.2g; Cholesterol 100mg; Calcium 214mg; Fibre 0.2g; Sodium 288mg.

Hot crab soufflés

These delicious little soufflés must be served as soon as they are ready, so seat your guests at the table before taking the soufflés out of the oven. Use local freshly caught crabs if possible, although canned or frozen will do if necessary.

Serves 6

50g/2oz/¼ cup butter

45ml/3 tbsp fine wholemeal (whole-wheat) breadcrumbs

4 spring onions (scallions), finely chopped

15ml/1 tbsp Malaysian or mild Madras curry powder

25g/1oz/¼ cup plain (all-purpose) flour

105ml/7 tbsp coconut milk or milk

150ml/¼ pint/⅔ cup whipping cream

4 eggs, separated, plus 2 extra egg whites

225g/8oz white crab meat

mild green Tabasco sauce, to taste

salt and ground black pepper

1 Use a little of the butter to grease six ramekins or a 1.75 litre/3 pint/7½ cup soufflé dish. Sprinkle in the fine wholemeal breadcrumbs, roll the dish(es) around to coat the base and sides completely, then tip out the excess breadcrumbs. Preheat the oven to 200°C/400°F/Gas 6.

2 Melt the remaining butter in a pan, add the spring onions and Malaysian or mild Madras curry powder and cook over a low heat for about 1 minute, until softened. Stir in the flour and cook for 1 minute more.

3 Gradually add the coconut milk or milk and cream, stirring continuously until each batch is thoroughly absorbed. Cook over a low heat until the mixture is smooth and thick.

4 Off the heat, stir in the egg yolks, then the crab meat. Season with salt, black pepper and Tabasco sauce.

5 In a grease-free bowl, beat the egg whites stiffly with a pinch of salt. Using a metal spoon, stir one-third into the crab mixture to lighten it; fold in the rest. Spoon into the dish(es).

6 Bake in the preheated oven until well risen and golden brown, and firm to the touch. Individual soufflés will be ready in 8 minutes; a large soufflé will take 15–20 minutes. Serve immediately.

Variation
Lobster or salmon can be used instead of crab in these soufflés. Cook the fish before adding it to the mixture.

Per portion Energy 234kcal/972kJ; Protein 11.8g; Carbohydrate 8.7g, of which sugars 1.8g; Fat 17.1g, of which saturates 9.3g; Cholesterol 97mg; Calcium 37mg; Fibre 0.3g; Sodium 322mg.

Main courses

Traditional Scottish cuisine tends to feature
prime cuts of meat, poultry or game, either in
everyday pies and stews or with sumptuous
sauces using local ingredients. Fish and shellfish
are also widely enjoyed, and the rivers, loch and
sea are full of superb wild fish, lobsters, crabs
and prawns. Choose from luscious Grilled
Lobster with Tarragon Cream, exquisite Halibut
with Leek and Ginger, comforting Dundee Beef
Stew, and succulent Roast Young Grouse.

King scallops with bacon

This is the simplest of dishes, combining bacon and scallops with brown butter which has just begun to burn but not quite. It gives a tasty dish and has a lovely aroma, which is why the French call this dish "noisette" – nutty.

Serves 4

12 rashers (strips) streaky (fatty) bacon

12 scallops

225g/8oz/1 cup unsalted (sweet) butter

juice of 1 lemon

30ml/2 tbsp chopped fresh flat leaf parsley

ground black pepper

1 Preheat the grill (broiler) to high. Wrap a rasher of bacon around each scallop so it goes over the top and not round the side.

2 Cut the butter into chunks and put it in a small pan over a low heat.

3 Meanwhile grill (broil) the scallops with the bacon facing up so it protects the meat. The bacon fat will help to cook the scallops. This will take only a few minutes; once they are cooked set aside and keep warm.

4 Allow the butter to turn a nutty brown colour, gently swirling it from time to time. Just as it is foaming and darkening, take off the heat and add the lemon juice. Be warned, it will bubble up quite dramatically.

5 Place the scallops on warmed plates, dress with plenty of chopped fresh parsley and pour the butter over.

Cook's Tip
Get the scallops on to warmed plates just as the butter is coming to the right colour, then add the lemon juice.

Per portion Energy 665kcal/2749kJ; Protein 24.4g; Carbohydrate 2.7g, of which sugars 0.6g; Fat 62g, of which saturates 34.7g; Cholesterol 189mg; Calcium 51mg; Fibre 0.5g; Sodium 1240mg.

Steamed mussels with spinach salsa

Mussels are an under-used shellfish, and have the advantages of combining well with lots of different flavours and being quite inexpensive compared to other kinds of seafood. The colours of this dish are pretty if you leave the mussels in the half-shell.

Serves 4

64 mussels

4 bunches fresh spinach

8 ripe tomatoes, blanched and peeled

2 spring onions (scallions), finely chopped

dash of white wine

For the salsa

120ml/4fl oz/½ cup olive oil

2 garlic cloves, crushed

30ml/2 tbsp chopped fresh coriander (cilantro)

115g/4oz/½ cup butter

salt and ground black pepper

1 Clean the mussels using a hard brush or a small, sharp knife. Remove any beards from the outside and discard any mussels with broken shells or that are open. Leave them to soak in a bowl of fresh slightly salted cold water for at least 30 minutes before cooking.

2 Wash the spinach thoroughly and remove the stalks. Cut the tomatoes into quarters, remove the seeds and dice finely.

3 Put the mussels and spring onion into a pan, add the wine and cover. Steam for a few minutes until the shells open then remove from the pan and leave to cool. Discard any that remain closed.

4 Meanwhile, make the salsa. Place the juices that were used to steam the mussels in a bowl and whisk them together with the oil to create an emulsion, then add the tomatoes, garlic and coriander.

5 To assemble, break off one shell and loosen the mussel in the other. Cook the spinach in a frying pan with the butter until just wilting (then season with salt and ground black pepper. Distribute among four warmed plates, arrange the shelled mussels on top and spoon over the salsa.

Per portion Energy 258kcal/1070kJ; Protein 9g; Carbohydrate 4.6g, of which sugars 4.5g; Fat 22.8g, of which saturates 8.4g; Cholesterol 42mg; Calcium 181mg; Fibre 2.4g; Sodium 244mg.

Grilled lobster with tarragon cream

Lobsters are readily available in Scotland; look out for them in the fishmongers in fishing villages, as you can choose your own live lobster, freshly caught that day. Lobsters are at their best prepared simply to make the most of their firm sweet meat. Fresh herbs, cream and melted butter are among the most suitable accompaniments.

Serves 4

2 live lobsters, approximately 675–800g/1½–1¾lb

grated rind of 1 orange

75g/3oz/6 tbsp unsalted (sweet) butter

pinch of cayenne pepper

50ml/2fl oz/¼ cup whipping cream

2 sprigs of fresh tarragon

salt and ground black pepper

1 Dispatch or freeze the lobsters before cooking, if you like (see Cook's Tip), then bring a large pan of water to the boil over a high heat. Add the grated orange rind and plunge the whole lobsters into the pan. Bring the water back to a rolling boil then boil for about 5 minutes.

2 Drain the lobsters and leave to cool. Once cooled, split the lobsters in two down the middle with a sharp knife. Remove the stomach sac from the head and the intestine tract, which runs down the tail. Remove the claws and crack them open. Remove the meat and place it in the head.

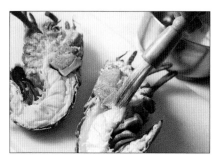

3 Melt the butter and brush it liberally over the four half lobsters, covering all the exposed flesh. Season lightly with salt and a little cayenne pepper.

4 Preheat the grill (broiler) to high. Pour the cream into a pan over a low heat and add the sprigs of tarragon, stirring it in gently. Bring the cream to just below boiling point, turn the heat right down and then leave the cream to infuse the flavours and aromas of the tarragon for 10 minutes.

Cook's Tip

If you are worried about dispatching a live lobster then either plunge a small sharp knife through the back of its head prior to boiling or place it in the deep freeze for 20 minutes before boiling; the cold makes them sleepy and they don't feel the heat as they are plunged into the pan of water.

5 Put the lobsters under the preheated grill for about 7 minutes and then pour off the juices into the cream and tarragon. Stir them in gently.

6 Add the buttery lobster juices from the grill pan and turn the heat up a fraction. Bring the cream mixture to the boil, whisking to combine the buttery lobster juices with the tarragon cream. Strain the sauce.

7 Place half a lobster on each warmed serving plate, and gently spoon over the cream sauce, letting it spill over on to the plate. Serve immediately.

Variation

Lobster also goes well with other fresh herbs. Wild garlic works well for this dish; use a few sprigs in the same way as the tarragon. Fresh dill also gives a lovely flavour. Chop it finely before adding it to the cream.

Per portion Energy 284kcal/1180kJ; Protein 20.8g; Carbohydrate 0.8g, of which sugars 0.8g; Fat 22.1g, of which saturates 13.2g; Cholesterol 153mg; Calcium 91mg; Fibre 0.6g; Sodium 421mg.

Squid with tomato and Strathdon Blue salsa

Squid is landed at the west-coast ports of Scotland and is often simply grilled. The use of tomatoes and a local Aberdeen cheese takes this delicacy to a different level.

2 Mix the avocado with the tomatoes, shallots and chilli, and combine with the measured virgin olive oil.

3 Spoon the salsa in mounds on to four individual plates.

4 Heat a griddle pan or a heavy pan. Brush the squid with olive oil and put straight into the pan, pushing it down gently. After a couple of minutes, turn it over and push down again.

5 When cooked, place the squid on top of the salsa, scatter over the diced cheese and then sprinkle with a little virgin olive oil and lemon juice. Serve immediately.

Serves 4

2 avocados

450g/1lb very ripe tomatoes, roughly chopped

2 shallots, chopped

1 red chilli, seeded and finely chopped

15ml/1 tbsp virgin olive oil, plus extra for sprinkling

900g/2lb prepared squid

115g/4oz Strathdon Blue cheese, diced

a little olive oil

a little lemon juice

1 To make the salsa, peel the avocados and remove the stones (pits). You can do this by cutting the fruits first in half and stabbing the stone (pit) with a kife to draw it out. Then cut each half lengthways to make quarters and simply peel the skin back from each slice. You may need to use a small knife. Cut the fruit into small cubes.

Cook's Tips
• Ask your fishmonger to do all the hard work of cleaning and skinning for you so you receive a piece of squid cut in half and ready to grill quickly.
• The squid may be cooked on the barbecue if you like.

Per portion Energy 421kcal/1762kJ; Protein 42.2g; Carbohydrate 8.3g, of which sugars 4.6g; Fat 24.5g, of which saturates 8.7g; Cholesterol 527mg; Calcium 181mg; Fibre 3g; Sodium 597mg.

Salmon fishcakes

The secret of a good fishcake is to make it with freshly prepared fish and potatoes, homemade breadcrumbs and plenty of interesting seasoning.

Serves 4

450g/1lb cooked salmon fillet

450g/1lb freshly cooked potatoes, mashed

25g/1oz/2 tbsp butter, melted

10ml/2 tsp wholegrain mustard

15ml/1 tbsp each chopped fresh dill and chopped fresh flat leaf parsley

grated rind and juice of ½ lemon

15g/½oz/1 tbsp plain (all-purpose) flour

1 egg, lightly beaten

150g/5oz/generous 1 cup dried breadcrumbs

60ml/4 tbsp sunflower oil

salt and ground white pepper

rocket (arugula) leaves and fresh chives, to garnish

lemon wedges, to serve

1 Flake the cooked salmon, watching carefully for and discarding any skin and bones. Place the flaked salmon in a bowl with the mashed potato, melted butter and wholegrain mustard. Mix well then stir in the chopped fresh dill and parsley, lemon rind and juice. Season to taste.

2 Divide the mixture into eight portions and shape each into a ball, then flatten into a thick disc. Dip the fish cakes first in flour, then in egg and finally in breadcrumbs, making sure they are evenly coated.

3 Heat the oil in a frying pan until very hot. Fry the fishcakes in batches until golden brown and crisp all over. As each batch is ready, drain on kitchen paper and keep hot.

4 Warm some plates and then place two fishcakes on to each warmed plate, one slightly on top of the other. Garnish with rocket leaves and chives, and serve with lemon wedges.

Cook's Tip
Almost any fresh white or hot-smoked fish is suitable; smoked cod and haddock are particularly good. A mixture of smoked and unsmoked fish also works well.

Per portion Energy 586kcal/2453kJ; Protein 29.8g; Carbohydrate 49.9g, of which sugars 3.2g; Fat 31g, of which saturates 7.2g; Cholesterol 117mg; Calcium 79mg; Fibre 1.3g; Sodium 266mg.

Coulibiac

Wild salmon was very plentiful in Scotland in the 19th century, although the rise in gaming and fishing led to an Act of Parliament being passed banning the gentry from feeding their staff on salmon more than three times a week. This wonderful pie was probably one of the ways in which the staff would enjoy it.

Serves 4

50g/2oz/¼ cup butter

1 small onion, finely chopped

175g/6oz/scant 1 cup long grain rice

350ml/12fl oz/1½ cups chicken stock

1 bay leaf

olive oil

175g/6oz button (white) mushrooms

450g/1lb ready-made puff pastry

2.25kg/5lb salmon, skinned and filleted

dash of dry white wine

chopped fresh fennel

3 eggs, boiled until firm and sliced

egg wash, made by whisking 1 egg with a little milk

salt and ground black pepper

For the hollandaise sauce

3 egg yolks

30ml/2 tbsp white wine vinegar

115g/4oz/½ cup butter, diced

1.5ml/¼ tsp salt

pinch of ground black pepper

1 Preheat the oven to 180°C/350°F/ Gas 4. In a small ovenproof pan, melt half the butter then cook the onion until translucent. Add the rice and stir. Add the stock and a pinch of salt. Bring to the boil and add the bay leaf. Cover and cook in the preheated oven for 20 minutes. When cooked gently fluff up the rice with a fork and leave to cool.

2 Slice the mushrooms finely. Heat the remaining butter with a little olive oil in a second pan and quickly fry the mushrooms. Set aside to cool.

3 Roll out the puff pastry into a square, long enough for a fillet and leaving 2.5cm/1in at each end. Sprinkle half the rice in a strip across the centre of the pastry. Cover with one salmon fillet, moisten with a little wine then season with salt and ground black pepper, and sprinkle over the chopped fresh fennel.

4 Cover the salmon with half the sliced egg and half the cooked mushrooms and a few spoonfuls of the rice. Then lay the second salmon fillet on top, adding another splash of wine and seasoning again with salt and ground black pepper. Place another layer of sliced egg over the top, sprinkle the rest of the mushrooms over, and finish by adding the remaining rice.

5 Brush the edges of the pastry with the egg wash, fold the pastry over and seal. Decorate with any pastry trimmings, if you like, and brush egg wash all over.

6 Allow to rest in a cool place for an hour. Meanwhile preheat the oven to 220°C/425°F/Gas 7. Bake the coulibiac in the preheated oven for about 40 minutes. If the pastry browns too quickly, turn down the heat. Allow to rest for 10 minutes before serving.

7 Make the hollandaise sauce. Put the egg yolks and vinegar in the top of a double boiler. Stir until thoroughly combined. Place the pan on the base pan filled with hot, but not boiling, water and heat gently, stirring, until the yolks begins to thicken. Add a piece of butter and whisk over a gentle heat until the butter has melted. Gradually add the remaining butter, whisking until the sauce thickens. Remove from the heat and stir in the salt and ground black pepper.

8 Use a serrated bread knife to cut the coulibiac and slice across its width. Hot and moist, it is delicious served with salad or a green vegetable with the hollandaise sauce. It is also excellent cold with a fresh salad.

Per portion Energy 1005kcal/4190kJ; Protein 50.7g; Carbohydrate 77.9g, of which sugars 2.4g; Fat 56.6g, of which saturates 7.8g; Cholesterol 244mg; Calcium 139mg; Fibre 0.7g; Sodium 521mg.

Halibut with leek and ginger

Generally fish needs to be absolutely fresh, but halibut needs to mature for a day or two to bring out the flavour. Halibut is normally taken from the Atlantic, but some of the boats on the east coast of Scotland will catch smaller ones, bringing in a catch so fresh you need to refrigerate the fish for a day or so before cooking.

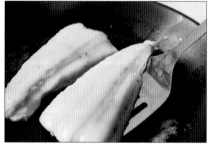

3 Dry the halibut steaks on kitchen paper. Heat a large pan with the olive oil and add 50g/2oz/¼ cup of the butter. As it begins to bubble place the fish steaks carefully in the pan, skin side down. Allow the halibut to colour – this will take 3–4 minutes. Then turn the steaks over, reduce the heat and cook for about a further 10 minutes.

Serves 4

2 leeks

50g/2oz piece fresh root ginger

4 halibut steaks, approximately 175g/6oz each (see Cook's Tip)

15ml/1 tbsp olive oil

75g/3oz/6 tbsp butter

Cook's Tips

• Ask your fishmonger for flattish halibut steaks and not too thick as you want to cook them in a pan on the stove and not in the oven. Also ask him or her to skin them for you.
• It doesn't matter if you leave a bit of skin on the ginger if it is very knobbly.

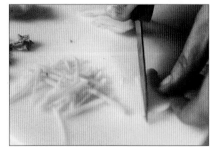

1 Trim the leeks, discarding the coarse outer leaves, the very dark green tops and the root end. Cut them into 5cm/2in lengths then slice into thin matchsticks. Wash thoroughly.

2 Peel the fresh ginger as best you can then slice it very thinly and cut the slices into thin sticks.

4 Remove the fish from the pan, set aside and keep warm. Add the leek and ginger to the pan, stir to mix then allow the leek to soften (they may colour slightly but this is fine). Once softened, season with a little salt and ground black pepper. Cut the remaining butter into small pieces then, off the heat, gradually stir into the pan.

5 To serve, place the halibut steaks on individual warmed plates and strew the leek and ginger mixture over the fish. Accompany with mashed potato.

Per portion Energy 364kcal/1520kJ; Protein 39.1g; Carbohydrate 2.7g, of which sugars 2.1g; Fat 21.9g, of which saturates 10.8g; Cholesterol 101mg; Calcium 75mg; Fibre 1.9g; Sodium 221mg.

Crusted garlic and wild thyme monkfish

Monkfish is a lovely juicy fish; it is hard to believe that until recently it was thrown back into the sea or sold breaded as "scampi" because its firm texture was not fashionable. Now it is considered a prime fish that needs simple cooking. Garlic is excellent with it, as are aromatic herbs such as wild thyme and fennel.

Serves 4

4 monkfish tails (see Cook's Tip)

garlic and herb butter (see Langoustines with Garlic Butter, but use wild thyme or bog myrtle in place of parsley)

115g/4oz/generous 1 cup dried breadcrumbs (see Cook's Tip)

salt and ground black pepper

2 Season the fish with salt and freshly ground black pepper. Using your fingertips, rub the garlic butter liberally all over, ensuring that you have pushed a good quantity into each of the diagonal slashes.

3 Sprinkle on the breadcrumbs, place on a baking tray and bake for 10–15 minutes. The cooked tails should be golden brown, with white slashes where the cuts have opened up to reveal the succulent flesh inside.

1 Preheat the oven to 220°C/425°F/ Gas 7. Make two or three diagonal slashes down each side of the fish, working from the bone to the edge.

Cook's Tips
• Buy monkfish tails weighing about 250g/9oz each. Ask your fishmonger to trim off all the skin and purple membrane surrounding the fillets but to leave the fish on the bone.
• The best breadcrumbs are made with day-old bread. Break the bread up with your fingers and then roughly in a food processor to make coarse breadcrumbs. Leave to dry out further overnight. The next day process the dried bread again to obtain fine dry crumbs. If you are really fussy you can then pass them through a coarse sieve to produce a very fine crumb.

Per portion Energy 272kcal/1130kJ; Protein 11.4g; Carbohydrate 9.9g, of which sugars 0.5g; Fat 21.1g, of which saturates 13.1g; Cholesterol 62mg; Calcium 26mg; Fibre 0.3g; Sodium 258mg.

Gratin of cod with wholegrain mustard

While the cod crisis continues in Scottish waters, cooks in north-west Europe are advised not to eat Atlantic cod. However, you can now buy good-quality farmed cod and elsewhere in the world cod or its local equivalents are still available.

Serves 4

4 cod steaks, approximately 175g/6oz each

200g/7oz/1¾ cups grated Cheddar cheese, such as Isle of Mull

15ml/1 tbsp wholegrain mustard

75ml/5 tbsp double (heavy) cream

salt and ground black pepper

1 Preheat the oven to 200°C/400°F/ Gas 6. Check the fish for bones. Butter the base and sides of an ovenproof dish then place the fish fillets skin side down in the dish and season.

2 In a small bowl, mix the grated cheese and mustard together with enough cream to form a spreadable but thick paste. Make sure that the cheese and mustard are thoroughly blended to ensure an even taste. Season lightly with salt and ground black pepper.

3 Spread the cheese mixture thickly and evenly over each fish fillet, using it all up. Bake in the preheated oven for 20 minutes. The top will be browned and bubbling and the fish underneath flaky and tender. Serve immediately on warmed plates.

Per portion Energy 445kcal/1852kJ; Protein 46g; Carbohydrate 0.4g, of which sugars 0.4g; Fat 27.7g, of which saturates 17.3g; Cholesterol 157mg; Calcium 395mg; Fibre 0g; Sodium 474mg.

West coast fisherman's stew

Many of the little ports on the west coast of Scotland still land a small catch and often there will be a box of bits and pieces, perhaps a monkfish or some small haddock, a few prawns and small crabs. Therein lies a feast waiting to be made.

Serves 4

30ml/2 tbsp olive oil

1 large onion, roughly chopped

1 leek, roughly chopped

2 garlic cloves, crushed

450g/1lb ripe tomatoes, roughly chopped

5ml/1 tsp tomato purée (paste)

1.3kg/3lb fish bones

a piece of pared orange peel

a few parsley stalks and fennel fronds

1 bay leaf

250ml/8fl oz/1 cup dry white wine

whisky or pastis, such as Pernod (optional)

1kg/2¼lb mixed fish fillets, such as salmon, sole and haddock, cut into chunks, and prepared shellfish

salt and ground black pepper

chopped fresh parsley, to garnish

2 Put in the fish bones, orange peel, herbs and wine, and add a little salt and ground black pepper. Then add enough water just to cover. Bring to a gentle boil then reduce the heat and simmer for 30 minutes.

3 Strain the soup into a clean pan, pressing the juices out of the solid ingredients with the back of a spoon.

4 Bring the liquid back to the boil and check for seasoning and texture. If you like, add a splash of whisky or Pernod. The fish takes just minutes to cook so add the firmer, larger pieces first, such as monkfish or salmon and mussels in the shell, and end with delicate scallops or prawn (shrimp) tails. Do not allow the stew to boil once you add the fish.

5 Serve in warmed soup plates, garnished with chopped fresh parsley.

1 Heat the olive oil in a large pan then sweat the onion and leek until soft. Add the garlic, tomatoes and tomato purée, and cook for 5 minutes.

Per portion Energy 341kcal/1432kJ; Protein 47.5g; Carbohydrate 6.5g, of which sugars 5.8g; Fat 7.8g, of which saturates 1.2g; Cholesterol 115mg; Calcium 53mg; Fibre 2.3g; Sodium 165mg.

Haggis with clapshot cake

Haggis is probably the best known of all Scottish dishes, not least because of the famous Burns poem which is recited the world over in front of a haggis at suppers celebrating the poet. This is the traditional haggis recipe served with turnip and potato clapshot – a variation on the "haggis with neeps and tatties" theme.

Serves 4

1 large haggis, approximately 800g/1¾lb

450g/1lb peeled turnip or swede (rutabaga)

225g/8oz peeled potatoes

120ml/4fl oz/½ cup milk

1 garlic clove, crushed with 5ml/1 tsp salt

175ml/6fl oz/¾ cup double (heavy) cream

freshly grated nutmeg

ground black pepper

butter, for greasing

1 Preheat the oven to 180°C/350°F/ Gas 4. Wrap the haggis in foil, covering it completely and folding over the edges of the foil.

Cook's Tip
If you are serving haggis on Burns Night (January 25th), you need to bring the haggis whole to the table on a platter and cut it open reciting the famous Burns poem. This is done in honour of Robert Burns, the celebrated Scottish poet.

2 Place the haggis in a roasting pan with about 2.5cm/1in water. Heat through in the preheated oven for 30–40 minutes.

3 Slice the turnip or swede and potatoes quite finely. A mandolin or food processor is quite handy for the turnip or swede as both vegetables tend to be hard and difficult to cut finely with a knife.

4 Put the sliced vegetables in a large pan and add the milk and garlic. Stir gently and continuously over a low heat until the potatoes begin to break down and exude their starch and the liquid thickens slightly.

5 Add the cream and nutmeg and grind some black pepper into the mixture. Stir gently but thoroughly. Slowly bring to the boil, reduce the heat and simmer gently for a few minutes.

6 Butter a deep round 18cm/7in dish or a small roasting pan. Transfer the vegetable mixture to the dish or pan. It shouldn't come up too high as it will rise slightly and bubble.

7 Bake in the oven for about 1 hour, or until you can push a knife easily through the cake. The top should be nicely browned by this time. If it is becoming too brown on top, cover it with foil and continue baking. If it is not browned enough after 1 hour of cooking, place it under a hot grill (broiler) for a few minutes.

8 Remove the foil from the haggis, place on a warmed serving dish and bring out to the table for your guests to witness the cutting. Use a sharp knife to cut through the skin then spoon out the haggis on to warmed plates. Serve the clapshot cake in slices with the haggis, spooning any juices over.

Per portion Energy 918kcal/3819kJ; Protein 24.9g; Carbohydrate 55.3g, of which sugars 8.5g; Fat 67.9g, of which saturates 30.2g; Cholesterol 244mg; Calcium 180mg; Fibre 3.1g; Sodium 1586mg.

Fillet steak with pickled walnut sauce

This is a traditional way of cooking beef, which makes it go a little further with the use of the onions. Fillet mignons are the small pieces from the end of the fillet, known as "collops" in Scotland. If you prefer, you can use Mushroom Sauce instead of pickled walnuts.

Serves 4

15ml/1 tbsp vegetable oil

75g/3oz/6 tbsp butter

8 slices of beef fillet (fillet mignon)

4 onions, sliced

15ml/1 tbsp pickled walnut juice

salt and ground black pepper

1 Heat the oil and half the butter in a frying pan and cook the steaks until almost done. Keep them warm.

2 Once you have taken your steaks out of the pan, melt the remaining butter then add the sliced onions. Increase the heat and stir to brown and soften the onions, scraping the base of the pan.

3 Add the pickled walnut juice and cook for a few minutes. Season to taste with salt and ground black pepper. Serve the beef on warmed plates and spoon the onions and juices over.

Per portion Energy 490kcal/2036kJ; Protein 43.4g; Carbohydrate 6.1g, of which sugars 4.3g; Fat 32.6g, of which saturates 17g; Cholesterol 167mg; Calcium 31mg; Fibre 1.1g; Sodium 219mg.

Dundee beef stew

The red wine quite possibly came into Dundee's busy port even though the majority must have come into Leith, the larger port for Edinburgh further south. This stew is excellent served with warming creamy mashed potatoes.

Serves 4

900g/2lb stewing beef

50g/2oz/½ cup plain (all-purpose) flour

2.5ml/½ tsp paprika

30ml/2 tbsp vegetable oil

225g/8oz onions, peeled and chopped

50g/2oz/½ stick butter

100g/4oz button (white) mushrooms, quartered

2 garlic cloves, crushed with a little salt

15ml/1 tbsp bitter marmalade

300ml/½ pint/1¼ cups red wine

150ml/¼ pint/⅔ cup beef stock

salt and ground black pepper

1 Preheat the oven to 180°C/350°F/ Gas 4. Then cut the meat into 2.5cm/1in cubes. Season the flour with some salt, ground black pepper and the paprika, spread it on a tray and coat the meat in it.

3 Transfer the meat to a casserole. Brown the onions in the original pan, adding a little butter if they seem too dry. Add to the casserole.

2 Heat a large pan, add the vegetable oil and brown the meat. Do this in batches if your pan is small.

4 Keeping the pan hot, add the rest of the butter and brown the mushrooms then transfer to the casserole.

5 Add the rest of the ingredients to the casserole and bring to the boil, stirring to combine the marmalade and evenly distribute the meat and mushrooms. Cover the casserole and place in the preheated oven for about 3 hours, until the meat is tender. Serve with creamy mashed potatoes.

Per portion Energy 544kcal/2276kJ; Protein 53.3g; Carbohydrate 17.1g, of which sugars 6.2g; Fat 24.1g, of which saturates 10.4g; Cholesterol 177mg; Calcium 53mg; Fibre 1.5g; Sodium 242mg.

Collops of beef with shallots

Beef is often paired with the sweetness of onions – a combination you will find time and again in traditional Scottish cooking. In this dish whole caramelized shallots are being used, giving a wonderful texture and flavour to the meal.

Serves 4

4 fillet steaks (beef tenderloin)

15ml/1 tbsp olive oil

50g/2oz/¼ cup butter

20 shallots, peeled

5ml/1 tsp caster (superfine) sugar

150ml/¼ pint/⅔ cup beef stock

salt and ground black pepper

1 Take the steaks out of the refrigerator well before you need them and dry with kitchen paper. Heat the oil and butter in a large frying pan then cook the steaks as you like them.

2 Once cooked remove the steaks from the pan and keep warm. Put the shallots in the pan and brown lightly in the meat juices. Add the sugar and then the stock. Reduce the heat to low and allow the liquid to evaporate, shaking the pan from time to time to stop the shallots from sticking.

3 The shallots will end up slightly soft, browned and caramelized with a shiny glaze. Season to taste with salt and ground black pepper.

4 Serve the steaks on warmed plates and spoon over the caramelized shallots and juices from the pan.

Per portion Energy 424kcal/1767kJ; Protein 43.2g; Carbohydrate 6.1g, of which sugars 4.6g; Fat 25.4g, of which saturates 12.5g; Cholesterol 149mg; Calcium 27mg; Fibre 0.9g; Sodium 166mg.

Mutton hotpot

A traditional cottage favourite, this mutton hotpot would have been a Sunday treat in the remote Highlands. Mutton is hard to come by today but it really is worth looking out for. Try your local farmers' market or ask your butcher if he could get it for you.

Serves 6

6 mutton chops

6 lamb's kidneys

1 large onion, sliced

450g/1lb potatoes, sliced

600ml/1 pint/2½ cups dark stock

salt and ground black pepper

1 Preheat the oven to 180°C/350°F/ Gas 4. Trim the mutton chops, leaving a little fat but no bone. Slice the kidneys in two horizontally and remove the fat and core with sharp scissors.

2 Place three of the chops in a deep casserole and season well with salt and ground black pepper.

3 Add a layer of half the kidneys, then half the onion and finally half the potatoes. Season lightly.

4 Repeat the process, seasoning as you go and making sure that you finish with an even layer of potatoes.

5 Heat the stock and pour it into the casserole, just about covering everything but leaving the potatoes just showing at the top. Cover and cook in the preheated oven for 2 hours, removing the lid for the last 30 minutes to allow the potatoes to brown.

Variation
If you prefer, you can use lamb chops instead. Use 2 chops per person and reduce the cooking time by 30 minutes as lamb does not need 2 hours.

Per portion Energy 626kcal/2629kJ; Protein 76.9g; Carbohydrate 23.1g, of which sugars 5g; Fat 25.8g, of which saturates 11.6g; Cholesterol 374mg; Calcium 76mg; Fibre 2g; Sodium 269mg.

Collops of venison with rowan sauce

Thickly sliced steaks makes a popular, easy-to-prepare and nutritious meal. Rowan berries come from the mountain ash, which grows all over Britain, parts of Europe and as a shade tree in the USA. The berries used here make a light red jelly with a sharp flavour that partners venison perfectly.

Serves 4

4 venison haunch steaks, about 200g/7oz each

15ml/1 tbsp vegetable oil

50g/2oz/¼ cup butter

15ml/1 tbsp rowan jelly

120ml/4fl oz/½ cup red wine

salt and ground black pepper

1 Bring the steaks out of the refrigerator a few hours prior to cooking, so that they will cook more quickly. Before cooking, dry the steaks on kitchen paper and season with salt and ground black pepper.

2 Heat a heavy pan and add the oil and half the butter. Cook the haunch steaks as you would a sirloin or fillet, browning both sides and then reducing the heat to complete the cooking.

3 When cooked to your liking, remove the steaks from the pan, set them aside and keep warm.

4 Mix together the rowan jelly and wine and then add to the pan, stirring to bring up the meat juices and dissolve the jelly. Once the jelly has melted, season the sauce with salt and ground black pepper then, off the heat, swirl in the remaining butter. Serve the steaks on warmed plates with the sauce poured over.

Per portion Energy 355kcal/1488kJ; Protein 44.5g; Carbohydrate 2.7g, of which sugars 2.7g; Fat 17.4g, of which saturates 8.4g; Cholesterol 127mg; Calcium 15mg; Fibre 0g; Sodium 189mg.

Roast venison

Venison has been eaten in Scotland for generations, by kings, lairds and ordinary people, hunted and poached in equal measure. Today the wild deer are culled regularly to keep the stocks healthy and excellent wild meat is available through game dealers. There are also a number of deer farms, which produce meat of a very high quality.

Serves 4

1 venison haunch, approximately 2.75kg/6lb

30ml/2 tbsp olive oil

25g/1oz/2 tbsp butter

225g/8oz bacon, diced

salt and ground black pepper

For the marinade

1 onion, sliced

2 carrots, peeled and sliced

60ml/4 tbsp olive oil

1 bottle red wine

2 garlic cloves, crushed

1 bay leaf

5 black peppercorns

sprig of rosemary

6 juniper berries

For the sauce

15ml/1 tbsp plain (all-purpose) flour

15ml/1 tbsp butter, softened

150ml/¼ pint/⅔ cup port

15ml/1 tbsp rowan jelly

1 Marinate the meat two days before cooking. Cook the onion and carrots in the olive oil, without allowing them to colour. Then put the mixture into a non-metallic container that is large enough to hold the venison. Add the other ingredients. Put the haunch in and leave for two days, turning regularly to coat all sides.

2 When ready to cook, preheat the oven to 160°C/325°F/Gas 3. Remove the haunch from the marinade and dry with kitchen paper.

3 Put a large casserole, into which the haunch will fit with the lid on, over a high heat and add the oil and butter. Brown the bacon and then the haunch, browning it all over.

4 In another pan, reduce the marinade by half by boiling it rapidly and then strain over the haunch. Cover and cook for 30 minutes per 450g/1lb. When cooked, remove and keep warm, covered in foil so it does not dry out.

5 Strain the juices into a pan and boil rapidly. Make a beurre manié by mixing the flour and butter together and whisk it into the boiling liquor. Simmer until reduced by half. Add the port and the rowan jelly, adjust the seasoning, if necessary, and serve.

Per portion Energy 978kcal/4132kJ; Protein 167.1g; Carbohydrate 11.1g, of which sugars 7.3g; Fat 25.2g, of which saturates 8.8g; Cholesterol 383mg; Calcium 52mg; Fibre 0.2g; Sodium 442mg.

Chicken with summer vegetables and tarragon

This is an all-in-the-pot dish, with the chicken cooking liquor providing the stock for the rest of the cooking and the sauce. Summer vegetables are wonderfully packed with flavour, and it is up to you to pick the selection you prefer.

Serves 4

1.8kg/4lb boiling fowl (stewing chicken)

1 onion, peeled, studded with 6 cloves

1 bay leaf

a sprig each of thyme and parsley

10 black peppercorns

12 small potatoes, washed

8 small shallots, peeled

vegetables of your choice, such as carrots, courgettes (zucchini), broad (fava) beans and peas

25g/1oz/2 tbsp butter

30ml/2 tbsp plain (all-purpose) flour

60ml/4 tbsp chopped fresh tarragon

1 Wash the chicken and dry with kitchen paper. Place in a large pan with the onion, bay leaf, thyme, parsley and peppercorns, with water to cover. Stir to mix in all the ingredients and bring to the boil over a high heat. Reduce the heat and simmer gently for 1½ hours. Skim off the froth occasionally as the bird is boiling and make sure the chicken is covered, topping up with water if necessary.

2 Meanwhile prepare all the vegetables and place them in rows on a tray in order of cooking time, from the longest to the shortest.

3 Once cooked remove the chicken from the pan and keep warm. Remove all the seasonings, either with a slotted spoon or by straining the mixture, then bring the cooking liquor back to the boil, skimming off any fat that may have appeared on the top.

4 Start to cook the vegetables in the liqour, putting the potatoes in first for a few minutes, then adding the shallots and carrots, if using, and finally the green vegetables that take no time at all – mangetouts, for example, should go in when the potatoes are cooked. When the vegetables are cooked, place the chicken on a serving dish and surround with all the vegetables.

5 In a small pan melt the butter, add the flour and stir to create a roux. Slowly add some liquor from the large pan until a sauce is created – about 600ml/1 pint/2½ cups – and allow to simmer for a few minutes to reduce down and strengthen the flavour. At the last moment stir in the chopped fresh tarragon then ladle the sauce over the chicken and vegetables. Bring to the table and serve immediately.

Per portion Energy 713kcal/2973kJ; Protein 51.2g; Carbohydrate 39.3g, of which sugars 13g; Fat 40g, of which saturates 12.9g; Cholesterol 261mg; Calcium 103mg; Fibre 5.4g; Sodium 251mg.

Roast young grouse

As with venison, rowan jelly goes well with this meat. Young grouse can be identified by their pliable breastbone, legs and feet, and their claws will be sharp. They have very little fat so bacon is used here to protect the breasts during the initial roasting.

Serves 2

2 young grouse

6 rashers (strips) bacon

2 sprigs of rowanberries or
1 lemon, quartered, plus
30ml/2 tbsp extra rowanberries
(optional)

50g/2oz/¼ cup butter

150ml/¼ pint/⅔ cup red wine

150ml/¼ pint/⅔ cup water

5ml/1 tsp rowan jelly

salt and ground black pepper

1 Preheat the oven to 200°C/400°F/ Gas 6. Wipe the grouse with kitchen paper and place in a roasting pan. Lay the bacon over the breasts.

2 If you have rowanberries, place one sprig in the cavity of each grouse as well as a little butter. Otherwise put a lemon quarter in each cavity.

3 Roast the grouse in the preheated oven for 10 minutes, then remove the bacon and pour in the wine. Return to the oven for 10 minutes.

4 Baste the birds with the juices and cook for a further 5 minutes. Remove the birds from the pan and keep warm. Add the water and rowan jelly to the pan and simmer gently until the jelly melts. Strain into another pan, add the rowanberries, if using, and simmer until the sauce just begins to thicken. Season with salt and ground black pepper.

Cook's Tip
Grouse is traditionally served with bread sauce and game chips but Skirlie is excellent too.

Per portion Energy 423kcal/1763kJ; Protein 43.8g; Carbohydrate 1.5g, of which sugars 1.5g; Fat 24g, of which saturates 10.8g; Cholesterol 51mg; Calcium 43mg; Fibre 0g; Sodium 902mg.

Pan-fried pheasant with oatmeal and cream sauce

Rolled oats are often used for coating fish before pan-frying, but this treatment is equally good with tender poultry, game and other meats. Sweet, slightly tangy redcurrant jelly is used to bind the oatmeal to the tender pheasant breast fillets.

Serves 4

115g/4oz/generous 1 cup medium rolled oats

4 skinless, boneless pheasant breasts

45ml/3 tbsp redcurrant jelly, melted

50g/2oz/¼ cup butter

15ml/1 tbsp olive oil

45ml/3 tbsp wholegrain mustard

300ml/½ pint/1¼ cups double (heavy) cream

salt and ground black pepper

1 Place the rolled oats on a plate and season with salt and ground black pepper. Brush the skinned pheasant breasts with the melted redcurrant jelly, then turn them in the oats to coat evenly. Shake off any excess oats and set aside.

2 Heat the butter and oil in a frying pan until foaming. Add the pheasant breasts and cook over a high heat, turning frequently, until they are golden brown on all sides. Reduce the heat to medium and cook for a further 8–10 minutes, turning once or twice, until the meat is thoroughly cooked.

3 Add the mustard and cream, stirring to combine with the cooking juices. Bring slowly to the boil then simmer for 10 minutes over a low heat, or until the sauce has thickened to a good consistency. Serve immediately.

Per portion Energy 847kcal/3520kJ; Protein 37.1g; Carbohydrate 30.1g, of which sugars 9.1g; Fat 59g, of which saturates 35.1g; Cholesterol 129mg; Calcium 105mg; Fibre 2g; Sodium 205mg.

Grey partridge with lentils and sausage

Grey partridge is indigenous to Scotland, although it is often called the English partridge, and is slightly smaller than the European red-legged variety. The wonderful rich flavour is complemented by the lovely earthy flavour of the Puy lentils.

Serves 4

450g/1lb/2 cups Puy lentils

75g/3oz/6 tbsp butter

15ml/1 tbsp vegetable oil

4 grey partridges

2 venison sausages

1 garlic clove, peeled but left whole

250ml/8fl oz/1 cup stock

salt and ground black pepper

1 Preheat the oven to 180°C/350°F/ Gas 4. Wash the lentils then simmer them in water for about 10 minutes to soften slightly. Drain then set aside.

2 Melt one-third of the butter with the oil in a large ovenproof frying pan and place the partridges, breast side down, in the pan. Brown both breasts lightly.

3 Set the partidges on their backs, season lightly with salt and ground black pepper and cook in the preheated oven for 15 minutes.

4 When cooked, remove the partridges from the oven, allow to cool for a few minutes then remove the legs. Keep the rest warm.

5 Put the large frying pan back on the hob and brown the two sausages. Add the Puy lentils and garlic and stir to coat in the juices from the partridges and the sausages. Then add the stock and simmer for a few minutes. Place the partidge legs on top of the lentil mixture and return to the oven for a further 15 minutes.

6 Remove the pan from the oven and set aside the partridge legs and sausages. Discard the garlic. Season the lentils with salt and ground black pepper, and if there is still a lot of liquid remaining, boil over a low heat to evaporate a little of the excess moisture. Then, off the heat, gradually swirl in the remaining butter.

7 Remove the breasts from the carcasses and set aside. Cut the sausages into pieces and stir into the lentil mixture.

8 To serve, place a leg on individual warmed plates, put the lentils on top and then the breast, sliced lengthways, on top of the lentils.

Per portion Energy 1309kcal/5495kJ; Protein 152.1g; Carbohydrate 59.4g, of which sugars 2.2g; Fat 53g, of which saturates 20.1g; Cholesterol 55mg; Calcium 255mg; Fibre 10.2g; Sodium 761mg.

Rabbit salad with ruby chard

Chard is a delicious vegetable and can be used in place of spinach in many recipes. The stalks are longer and thicker than spinach and the leaf has a great colour, especially the ruby varieties, which is a deep red. Prepare it as you would spinach. Rabbits are plentiful in Scotland and are a traditional favourite. This quick method is only good for the saddle.

4 Remove the rabbit from the pan and return the pan to the hob, add the butter and, as soon as it is melted, throw the chard in all at once. (It may be heaped up but will soon wilt down.) Season with salt and ground black pepper and toss to coat well with the butter. Once it has wilted – about 3 minutes – it is ready.

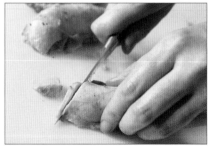

Serves 4

15ml/1 tbsp groundnut (peanut) oil

2 saddles of rabbit, each weighing approximately 250g/9oz

mixed salad leaves

salad dressing

50g/2oz/¼ cup butter

225g/8oz ruby chard leaves (stalks removed)

salt and ground black pepper

1 Heat a frying pan and pour in the oil, allowing it to get quite hot. Dry and season the saddles of rabbit and place them skin side down. Reduce the heat and brown lightly in the pan.

2 Turn the saddles over on to the rib side, cover and cook over a very low heat for about 7 minutes. Turn off the heat, and leave to rest.

3 Make a salad using colourful leaves. Toss with your dressing and place in the centre of four individual plates.

5 Slice the rabbit fillets from the back of the saddle and take the small fillets from underneath as well. Cut thinly and strew evenly over the salad. Place the warm chard on top and serve.

Cook's Tip
In Scotland the thick stalks of chard are often cut off and stirred into a white sauce as a separate side dish. Cut them off raw and steam them for 5–6 minutes then arrange on a serving dish and cover with a white sauce as you would do with asparagus.

Per portion Energy 287kcal/1192kJ; Protein 29g; Carbohydrate 1g, of which sugars 0.9g; Fat 18.5g, of which saturates 9.1g; Cholesterol 115mg; Calcium 126mg; Fibre 1.2g; Sodium 238mg.

Saddle of rabbit with asparagus

Some of the best asparagus comes from near Glamis in Angus in the east of the country where a little extra sunlight produces stems with juicy, succulent flavours. This is not like the white asparagus of Europe, which is grown underground, but a better-flavoured, more satisfying green variety, which grows above the soil.

Serves 4

2 saddles of rabbit

75g/3oz/6 tbsp butter

sprig of fresh rosemary

45ml/3 tbsp olive oil

10 asparagus spears

200ml/7fl oz/scant 1 cup chicken stock, plus extra for cooking the asparagus (see Step 5)

salt and ground black pepper

1 Preheat the oven to 200°C/400°F/ Gas 6. Trim the rabbit saddles, removing the membrane and the belly flaps.

2 Heat an ovenproof pan then add 50g/2oz/4 tbsp of the butter. Season the saddles and brown them lightly all over, by frying them gently in the butter for a few minutes on each side.

3 Tuck the rosemary underneath the saddles, with the fillets facing up, and put in the oven for 10 minutes.

4 Meanwhile, in a second pan, heat the olive oil then add the asparagus spears. Make sure they are coated in the oil and leave them to sweat gently for a few minutes.

5 Add enough stock to just cover the asparagus and bring to a gentle boil. Allow the liquid to evaporate to a light glaze and the asparagus will be cooked.

6 Remove the rabbit from the oven and leave to rest for 5 minutes. Remove any fat from the pan then add the measured stock. Bring to the boil, scraping up any bits from the base of the pan. Reduce the liquid by about a half, then remove from the heat and whisk in the remaining butter. Strain through a sieve and set aside.

7 Take the meat off the saddles in slices lengthways and place on a warmed serving dish. Serve with the asparagus on top and the sauce spooned over.

Per portion Energy 406kcal/1684kJ; Protein 33.7g; Carbohydrate 0.6g, of which sugars 0.6g; Fat 29.8g, of which saturates 13.4g; Cholesterol 146mg; Calcium 43mg; Fibre 0.4g; Sodium 215mg.

Loin of wild boar with bog myrtle

Wild boar used to roam the hills of Scotland centuries ago and when the kings of Scotland came for their summer holidays to Falkland Palace, Fife, they would go out hunting for them. Today they no longer exist in the wild but are farmed as a rare breed of pig. Their meat is similar to pork in that it has a sweetness to it, and the crackling is fantastic.

Serves 4

1 loin of wild boar, approximately 2.75kg/6lb

10ml/2 tsp salt

1 onion, roughly chopped

1 carrot, peeled and roughly chopped

150ml/¼ pint/⅔ cup dry vermouth

10ml/2 tsp English mustard

handful of bog myrtle, or a few sprigs of fresh rosemary, if you prefer

salt and ground black pepper

1 Ask your butcher to take the loin off the bone and then to tie it back on and to make 2cm/¾in cuts through the skin from top to bottom at 5cm/2in intervals. This will make the crackling easier to slice when you come to carve. Allow the loin to sit at room temperature for at least an hour prior to cooking. Preheat the oven to 220°C/425°F/Gas 7.

2 Rub the salt all over the skin of the boar, easing it slightly into the cuts made by the butcher.

3 Place the chopped vegetables and herbs in a lightly oiled roasting pan.

4 Put the loin on top of the vegetables and herbs, with the skin facing up, and roast in the oven for 40 minutes.

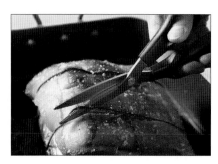

5 Reduce the oven temperature to 180°C/350°F/Gas 4 and cook for another 40 minutes. Remove from the oven and cut the meat from the bones – this should just be a matter of cutting the string. Set the meat aside to rest for at least 20 minutes.

6 Meanwhile make the gravy. Pour or spoon off the excess fat from the roasting pan but try to retain the juices, which will be under the fat.

7 Put the roasting pan on the stove over a low heat and add the vermouth and mustard. Stir well to mix thoroughly, scraping the base of the pan to incorporate the cooked flavours.

8 Just as it comes to the boil, pour the gravy into a clean pan, along with the bones, herbs and vegetables. Swill out the roasting pan with a little water and add this to the new pan, making sure that you have all the juices. Simmer the gravy in the new pan for about 5 minutes.

9 Remove the bones and strain the juices into the gravy pan. Test the seasoning, adding salt and ground black pepper if necessary.

10 Serve the loin in slices, each slice with a strip of the crackling, and pass around the gravy in a separate dish.

Cook's Tip
The crackling is particularly good and can be broken off in chunks because of the cuts made prior to cooking. The meat can be carved separately.

Per portion Energy 530kcal/2221kJ; Protein 81.9g; Carbohydrate 6.7g, of which sugars 5.7g; Fat 15.5g, of which saturates 5.3g; Cholesterol 236mg; Calcium 109mg; Fibre 1.9g; Sodium 1309mg.

Side dishes

Side dishes provide the healthy element to any traditional Scottish meal as they often include richly flavoured green vegetables. Potatoes are always a favourite, and oats are never too far away. This chapter contains a superb selection of popular vegetable dishes and accompaniments that will please any diner, including Skirlie, Cabbage with Bacon, Kale with Mustard Dressing and Celeriac Purée.

Kailkenny

This is a mashed potato combination dish, originating from the north-east of Scotland.
Normally the cabbage is boiled but it is more nutritious to quickly fry it, keeping in the
goodness. Kailkenny makes an excellent accompaniment to any meat dish.

Serves 4

450g/1lb potatoes, peeled
and chopped

50g/2oz/¼ cup butter

50ml/2fl oz/¼ cup milk

450g/1lb cabbage, washed and
finely shredded

30ml/2 tbsp olive oil

50ml/2fl oz/¼ cup double
(heavy) cream

salt and ground black pepper

1 Place the potatoes in boiling water
and boil for 15–20 minutes. Drain,
replace on the heat for a few minutes
then mash. Heat the butter and milk in
a small pan and then mix into the
mashed potatoes. Season to taste.

2 Heat the olive oil in a large frying
pan, add the shredded cabbage and fry
for a few minutes. Season to taste with
salt and ground black pepper. Add the
mashed potato, mix well then stir in the
cream. Serve immediately.

Per portion Energy 183kcal/766kJ; Protein 3.9g; Carbohydrate 24g, of which sugars 7.3g; Fat 8.5g, of which saturates 2.4g; Cholesterol 7mg; Calcium 73mg; Fibre 3.5g; Sodium 24mg.

Skirlie

Oatmeal has been a staple in Scotland for centuries. Skirlie is a simple preparation and can be used for stuffings or as an accompaniment, and is especially good with roast meats. It is traditionally cooked in lard but many people prefer butter.

Serves 4

50g/2oz/¼ cup butter

1 onion, finely chopped

175g/6oz/scant 2 cups medium rolled oats

salt and ground black pepper

Variation
To add a lovely rich flavour to the skirlie, grate in a little nutmeg and add a pinch of cinnamon towards the end.

1 Melt the butter in a pan over a medium heat and add the onion. Fry gently until it is softened and very slightly browned.

2 Stir in the rolled oats and season with salt and ground black pepper. Cook gently for 10 minutes. Taste for seasoning and serve immediately.

Per portion Energy 282kcal/1182kJ; Protein 6g; Carbohydrate 34.9g, of which sugars 2.2g; Fat 14.2g, of which saturates 6.5g; Cholesterol 27mg; Calcium 36mg; Fibre 3.5g; Sodium 91mg.

Cabbage with bacon

Bacon, especially if smoked, makes all the difference to the flavour of the cabbage, turning it into a delicious vegetable accompaniment to serve with roast beef, chicken or even a celebration turkey. Try it for people who don't like to eat greens.

Serves 4

30ml/2 tbsp oil

1 onion, finely chopped

115g/4oz smoked bacon, finely chopped

500g/1¼lb cabbage (red, white or Savoy)

salt and ground black pepper

1 Heat the oil in a large pan over a medium heat, add the chopped onion and bacon and cook for about 7 minutes, stirring occasionally.

2 Remove any tough outer leaves and wash the cabbages. Shred them quite finely, discarding the core. Add the cabbage to the pan and season. Stir for a few minutes until the cabbage begins to lose volume.

3 Continue to cook the cabbage, stirring frequently, for 8–10 minutes until it is tender but still crisp. (If you prefer softer cabbage, then cover the pan for part of the cooking time.) Serve immediately.

Variations
• This dish is equally delicious if you use spring greens (collards) instead of cabbage. You could also use curly kale.
• To make a more substantial dish to serve for lunch or supper, add more bacon, some chopped button (white) mushrooms and skinned, seeded and chopped tomatoes.

Per portion Energy 151kcal/623kJ; Protein 6.7g; Carbohydrate 7.4g, of which sugars 7g; Fat 10.5g, of which saturates 2.6g; Cholesterol 15mg; Calcium 67mg; Fibre 2.8g; Sodium 452mg.

Kale with mustard dressing

Traditionally, sea kale is used for this dish, available in Scotland between January and March. Its pale green fronds have a slightly nutty taste. Use curly kale if you can't get sea kale, although you will need to boil it briefly for a few minutes before chilling and serving.

Serves 4

250g/9oz sea kale or curly kale

45ml/3 tbsp light olive oil

5ml/1 tsp wholegrain mustard

15ml/1 tbsp white wine vinegar

pinch of caster (superfine) sugar

salt and ground black pepper

1 Wash the sea kale, drain thoroughly, then trim it and cut in two.

2 Whisk the oil into the mustard in a bowl. When it is blended completely, whisk in the white wine vinegar. It should begin to thicken.

3 Season the mustard dressing to taste with sugar, salt and ground black pepper. Toss the sea kale in the dressing and serve immediately.

Per portion Energy 99kcal/409kJ; Protein 2.1g; Carbohydrate 1.9g, of which sugars 1.9g; Fat 9.3g, of which saturates 1.3g; Cholesterol 0mg; Calcium 82mg; Fibre 2g; Sodium 27mg.

Young vegetables with tarragon

This is almost a salad, but the vegetables here are just lightly cooked to bring out their different flavours. The tarragon adds a wonderful depth to this bright, fresh dish. It goes well as a light accompaniment to fish and seafood dishes.

Serves 4

5 spring onions (scallions)

50g/2oz/¼ cup butter

1 garlic clove, crushed

115g/4oz asparagus tips

115g/4oz mangetouts (snowpeas), trimmed

115g/4oz broad (fava) beans

2 Little Gem (Bibb) lettuces

5ml/1 tsp finely chopped fresh tarragon

salt and ground black pepper

1 Cut the spring onions into quarters lengthways and fry gently over a medium-low heat in half the butter with the garlic.

2 Add the asparagus tips, mangetouts and broad beans. Mix in, covering all the pieces with oil.

3 Just cover the base of the pan with water, season, and allow to simmer gently for a few minutes.

4 Cut the lettuce into quarters and add to the pan. Cook for 3 minutes then, off the heat, swirl in the remaining butter and the tarragon, and serve.

Per portion Energy 149kcal/619kJ; Protein 4.7g; Carbohydrate 6.1g, of which sugars 3g; Fat 12g, of which saturates 7.3g; Cholesterol 29mg; Calcium 55mg; Fibre 3.5g; Sodium 89mg.

Celeriac purée

Celeriac is a most versatile vegetable which is ignored too often. This is sad as it is so good grated raw with mayonnaise and served with smoked salmon. Here it is made into a delicious purée that goes very well with game, poultry or roast pork or boar.

Serves 4

1 celeriac bulb, cut into chunks

1 lemon

2 potatoes, cut into chunks

300ml/½ pint/1¼ cups double (heavy) cream

salt and ground black pepper

chopped chives, to garnish

1 Place the celeriac in a pan. Cut the lemon in half and squeeze it into the pan, dropping the two halves in too.

2 Add the potatoes to the pan and just cover with cold water. Place a disc of greaseproof (waxed) paper over the vegetables. Bring to the boil, reduce the heat and simmer until tender, about 20 minutes.

3 Remove the lemon halves and drain through a colander. Return to the pan and allow to steam dry for a few minutes over a low heat.

4 Remove from the heat and purée in a food processor. This mixture can be set aside until you need it and can be kept in the refrigerator for a few days, covered with clear film (plastic wrap).

5 When ready to use, pour the cream into a pan and bring to the boil. Add the celeriac mixture and stir to heat through. Season, garnish wth snipped chives and serve.

Per portion Energy 403kcal/1661kJ; Protein 2.2g; Carbohydrate 7.9g, of which sugars 2.3g; Fat 40.5g, of which saturates 25.1g; Cholesterol 103mg; Calcium 65mg; Fibre 1.1g; Sodium 58mg.

Desserts and drinks

There are plenty of delicious traditional desserts
to enjoy, from creamy cold treats to rich fruit
tarts and hot puddings. The Scot's love of all
things sweet can only be matched by their love
of whisky – a quintessential Scottish drink. Its
history goes back centuries, to a time when it
was distilled by clans to enjoy with feasts.
Scotland has some superb drinks, many of which
use whisky as the base, both for everyday
enjoyment and also for special occasions.

Summer pudding

This traditional pudding is wonderfully easy to make, it is usually made with leftover breads and bannocks and a few handfuls of garden and hedgerow berries.

Serves 4–6

8 x 1cm/½in thick slices of day-old white bread, crusts removed

800g/1¾lb/6–7 cups mixed berries, such as strawberries, raspberries, blackcurrants, redcurrants and blueberries

50g/2oz/¼ cup golden caster (superfine) sugar

lightly whipped double (heavy) cream or crème fraîche, to serve

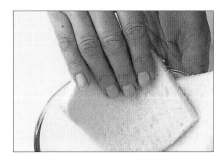

1 Trim a slice of bread to fit in the base of a 1.2 litre/2 pint/5 cup bowl, then trim another 5–6 slices to line the sides of the bowl, making sure the bread comes up above the rim.

2 Place all the fruit in a pan with the sugar. Do not add any water. Cook gently for 4–5 minutes until the juices begin to run.

3 Allow the mixture to cool then spoon the berries, and enough of their juices to moisten, into the bread-lined bowl. Reserve any remaining juice to serve with the pudding.

4 Fold over the excess bread from the side of the bowl, then cover the fruit with the remaining bread, trimming to fit. Place a small plate or saucer that fits inside the bowl directly on top of the pudding. Weight it down with a 900g/2lb weight, if you have one, or use a couple of full cans.

5 Chill the pudding in the refrigerator for at least 8 hours or overnight. To serve, run a knife between the pudding and the bowl and turn out on to a serving plate. Spoon any reserved juices over the top.

Per portion Energy 230kcal/977kJ; Protein 6.2g; Carbohydrate 51.7g, of which sugars 26.5g; Fat 1.2g, of which saturates 0g; Cholesterol 0mg; Calcium 98mg; Fibre 3g; Sodium 294mg.

Iced cranachan

Here is a wonderful way to enjoy cranachan. It is made into an ice cream with an oatmeal praline treatment and is delicious served with a fine Scottish shortbread.

Serves 4

115g/4oz/generous ½ cup caster (superfine) sugar

30ml/2 tbsp water

115g/4oz/1 cup pinhead oatmeal

6 egg whites

250g/9oz/1¼ cups caster (superfine) sugar

200ml/7fl oz/scant 1 cup double (heavy) cream

300ml/½ pint/1¼ cups single (light) cream

fresh raspberries, to garnish

1 Place the sugar and water in a pan and bring to the boil. When the mixture begins to turn golden brown stir in the oatmeal thoroughly and pour on to an oiled tray. When cool, crush into small pieces using a small rolling pin or a mortar and pestle. The oatmeal praline will keep refrigerated in an airtight jar for a week or more.

2 For the mousse, whisk the egg whites and sugar in a bowl over a pan of hot water until the sugar dissolves. Remove from the heat and whisk until cold, preferably using an electric whisk. Mix the creams together then whisk until they thicken slightly. Fold into the egg mixture and add the praline.

3 Pour into a loaf tin (pan) lined with clear film (plastic wrap), and freeze overnight.

4 To serve, turn out of the tin and peel off the clear film. Using a knife dipped in hot water, cut into slices. Garnish with fresh raspberries.

Per portion Energy 855kcal/3588kJ; Protein 11.1g; Carbohydrate 112.2g, of which sugars 94g; Fat 43.4g, of which saturates 25.8g; Cholesterol 110mg; Calcium 154mg; Fibre 1.7g; Sodium 138mg.

Rhubarb frushie

A frushie is the old Scots word for a crumble. In this instance the topping is made with coarse rolled oats. Other fruits, such as apple, blackberry or gooseberries, can also be used.

Serves 4

450g/1lb rhubarb or other fruit

50g/2oz/¼ cup caster (superfine) sugar or 30ml/2 tbsp redcurrant jelly

45–60ml/3–4 tbsp water

squeeze of lemon juice

For the crumble

50g/2oz/½ cup plain (all-purpose) flour

25g/1oz/scant ⅓ cup coarse rolled oats

50g/2oz/¼ cup soft light brown sugar

50g/2oz/¼ cup butter, softened

1 Preheat the oven to 200°C/400°F/ Gas 6. Cook the rhubarb or other fruit with the sugar or redcurrant jelly, water and lemon juice until soft but not mushy. Transfer to a deep pie dish.

2 Combine all the ingredients for the crumble with your fingers until the mixture has a crumb-like texture.

3 Sprinkle the crumble topping evenly over the fruit.

4 Bake at the top of the preheated oven for 20 minutes, or until the top is crunchy and slightly brown. Serve immediately with hot custard, fresh whipped cream or vanilla ice cream, if you like.

Per portion Energy 267kcal/1126kJ; Protein 3.2g; Carbohydrate 41.4g, of which sugars 27.3g; Fat 11.1g, of which saturates 6.5g; Cholesterol 27mg; Calcium 141mg; Fibre 2.4g; Sodium 83mg.

Dunfillan bramble pudding

This warming pudding comes from Dunfillan in Perthshire. It is easy to make, if you have a little time, and is perfect with fresh cream as a tasty dessert or teatime indulgence.

Serves 4

For the Dunfillan pastry

50g/2oz/¼ cup butter

50g/2oz/¼ cup caster (superfine) sugar

1 large egg, well beaten

115g/4oz/1 cup plain (all-purpose) flour, sifted

pinch of baking powder

30ml/2 tbsp milk

grated rind of 2 lemons

For the filling

450g/1lb/4 cups blackberries

75g/3oz/scant ½ cup caster (superfine) sugar

squeeze of lemon juice

sprinkling of cornflour (cornstarch)

1 Preheat the oven to 180°C/350°F/ Gas 4. Put the blackberries in a pan and barely cover with water, then add the sugar and lemon juice. Cook until soft, about 5 minutes.

2 Transfer the blackberries to an ovenproof dish in layers, sprinkling each layer with a little cornflour.

3 To make the pastry, cream the butter and sugar then add the beaten egg. Mix the flour and baking powder then add it alternately with the milk to the butter mixture, mixing well after each addition. Finally stir in the lemon rind.

4 Spread the pastry evenly over the fruit, taking small batches from the bowl and spreading carefully. Cook in the preheated oven for 20–30 minutes, or until the top is golden brown. Serve hot or cold.

Per portion Energy 366kcal/1539kJ; Protein 6.2g; Carbohydrate 60.2g, of which sugars 39.2g; Fat 12.8g, of which saturates 7.2g; Cholesterol 90mg; Calcium 122mg; Fibre 4.4g; Sodium 107mg.

Clootie dumpling

A rich, dense pudding, traditionally made in a "cloot", a cloth, then boiled in water over the fire. Clootie dumplings are traditionally made for the festive season.

Serves 8

225g/8oz/2 cups plain (all-purpose) flour, plus 15ml/1 tbsp for the cloot

115g/4oz/scant 1 cup suet (US chilled, grated shortening)

115g/4oz/generous 1 cup rolled oats

75g/3oz/scant ½ cup caster (superfine) sugar

5ml/1 tsp baking powder

225g/8oz/generous 1½ cups mixed sultanas (golden raisins) and currants

5ml/1 tsp each ground cinnamon and ground ginger

15ml/1 tbsp golden (light corn) syrup

2 eggs, lightly beaten

45–60ml/3–4 tbsp milk

1 Sift the flour into a dry bowl then add the suet to the flour. Using your fingertips, rub the fat into the flour until it is the texture of breadcrumbs. Add the rolled oats, sugar, baking powder, fruit and spices. Mix in well then add the syrup and eggs. Stir thoroughly, using enough milk to form a firm batter.

If using an ovenproof bowl
2 Lightly grease the inside of the bowl and put the mixture in, allowing at least 2.5cm/1in space at the top. Cover with baking parchment and tie down well.

3 Put an inverted plate or saucer in the base of a deep pan, place the dumpling on top and cover with boiling water. Cook for 2½–3 hours over a low heat.

If using a cloot
2 The cloot – or cloth – should be either cotton or linen, about 52cm/21in square. Plunge it into boiling water, remove it carefully from the pan, wring it out and lay it out on a flat surface.

3 Sprinkle 15ml/1 tbsp flour evenly over the cloot. Place the pudding mixture in the middle of the floured cloth then bring each of the four corners into the middle above the mixture and tie them up with a piece of strong, clean string, leaving plenty of space for the pudding to expand.

4 Either place in a bain-marie (a roasting pan filled with water and placed in the oven) or steam over a double boiler. Cook over a low heat for 2½–3 hours.

5 When the dumpling is cooked, turn out on to a large warmed plate. Serve in slices with hot jam and cream. It can also be eaten cold and will keep in an airtight container for a month.

Per portion Energy 902kcal/3798kJ; Protein 15.1g; Carbohydrate 143.3g, of which sugars 69.2g; Fat 35g, of which saturates 16.6g; Cholesterol 121mg; Calcium 183mg; Fibre 5.5g; Sodium 81mg.

Scone and butter pudding

The word scone originated in 16th-century Scotland. Scones are extremely easy to make but when you're short of time you may prefer to buy them from a bakery.

Serves 4

50g/2oz/scant ½ cup sultanas (golden raisins)

50g/2oz/¼ cup dried apricots, cut into small pieces

50ml/2fl oz/¼ cup whisky

300ml/½ pint/1¼ cups milk

300ml/½ pint/1¼ cups double (heavy) cream

5 egg yolks

50g/2oz/¼ cup caster (superfine) sugar

2 drops vanilla extract

6 scones

75g/3oz/6 tbsp butter

60ml/4 tbsp apricot jam, warmed

1 Place the dried fruit and whisky in a small glass bowl.

2 Cover and leave to soak overnight or for at least 2 hours. Preheat the oven to 200°C/400°F/Gas 6.

Cook's Tip
A bain-marie is a water bath used for cooking delicate dishes, such as custards. Place the ramekin dishes in a large, shallow pan of hot water before putting in the oven.

3 Whisk the milk, cream, egg yolks, sugar and vanilla extract. Slice the tops off the scones and then slice each into three rounds. Butter each round and then layer with the fruit and custard in buttered ramekins. Set aside for 1 hour.

4 Bake in a bain-marie (see Cook's Tip) in the preheated oven for 40 minutes until risen slightly and golden-brown in colour.

5 Remove from the oven and brush with the warmed apricot jam. Serve immediately in the ramekins, or carefully pass a small sharp knife around the inside of each and gently ease the puddings out into bowls or on to individual plates.

Variation
If you prefer, you can use Drambuie or brandy in place of the whisky.

Per portion Energy 796kcal/3305kJ; Protein 8.1g; Carbohydrate 43.2g, of which sugars 43.2g; Fat 63.9g, of which saturates 37.6g; Cholesterol 399mg; Calcium 178mg; Fibre 0.5g; Sodium 187mg.

Walnut and honey tart

Some of the best honey in the world comes from Scotland. Especially delicious is the honey made by bees that feed on wild heather, which is often found growing on the well-managed grouse moors. Serve this tart with plenty of whipped cream.

Serves 4

90g/3½oz sweet pastry

6 sugar cubes

200g/7oz/1¾ cups walnuts

75ml/5 tbsp good honey

45ml/3 tbsp double (heavy) cream

1 Preheat the oven to 200°C/400°F/ Gas 6. Roll the pastry out to a disc measuring about 25cm/10in across and allow to rest for 15 minutes. Place on a baking sheet then bake in the preheated oven for about 15 minutes.

2 Put the sugar and 60ml/4 tbsp water in a pan and heat until it caramelizes, stirring continuously. Add the walnuts and coat with caramel, toasting them lightly in the pan for a few minutes. Remove from the heat and allow to cool slightly.

3 Add the honey and cream, mixing thoroughly until the mixture has cooled completely.

4 Spread the walnut mixture over the pastry disc and rest for 10 minutes before serving.

Per portion Energy 563kcal/2338kJ; Protein 9.1g; Carbohydrate 35.9g, of which sugars 30.8g; Fat 43.5g, of which saturates 6.6g; Cholesterol 15mg; Calcium 70mg; Fibre 2g; Sodium 67mg.

Blackcurrant tart

Blackcurrants grow in the wild, are cultivated throughout Europe, and are widely available in North America. This tart makes the most of these exquisite summer fruits, and is quick and easy to prepare using ready-made puff pastry. Serve with whipped cream.

Serves 4

500g/1¼lb/5 cups blackcurrants

115g/4oz/generous ½ cup caster (superfine) sugar

250g/9oz ready-made puff pastry

50g/2oz/½ cup icing (confectioners') sugar

whipped cream, to serve

1 Preheat the oven to 220°C/425°F/ Gas 7. Trim the blackcurrants, making sure you remove all the stalks and any hard parts in the middle. Add the caster sugar and mix well.

2 Roll out the pastry to about 3mm/ ⅛in thick and cut out four discs roughly the size of a side plate or a large cereal bowl. Then using a smaller plate (or bowl) lightly mark with the point of a knife a circle about 2cm/¾in inside each disc.

3 Spread the blackcurrants over the discs, keeping them within the marked inner circle. Bake in the oven for 15 minutes. Dust generously with the icing sugar before serving. Serve hot with a large dollop of whipped cream, or serve cold as a teatime snack.

Per portion Energy 426kcal/1798kJ; Protein 4.9g; Carbohydrate 73.2g, of which sugars 50.9g; Fat 15.3g, of which saturates 0g; Cholesterol 0mg; Calcium 133mg; Fibre 4.5g; Sodium 200mg.

Prince Charlie's coffee

Bonnie Prince Charlie gave the recipe for Drambuie to the MacKinnon family, and it is now used to make this luxurious after-dinner coffee.

Serves 1

30ml/2 tbsp Drambuie

5ml/1 tsp soft light brown sugar

hot black coffee

50ml/2fl oz/¼ cup double (heavy) cream, lightly whipped

1 Pour the Drambuie into a tall wine glass with a 300ml/½ pint/1¼ cup capacity (as for the Highland Coffee). Add the sugar and stir thoroughly until completely dissolved.

2 Make a fresh pot of piping hot coffee – it is preferable to use either filter coffee or coffee made in a cafetière (press pot). It is also best to use a good, smooth coffee. Make it quite strong, although you don't want to smother the taste of the Drambuie completely.

3 Pour the hot coffee into the glass, leaving 2cm/¾in at the top, and stir.

4 Using a teaspoon with its tip just touching the coffee pour the lightly whipped cream over the coffee until it reaches the top of the glass.

Per portion Energy 90kcal/371kJ; Protein 0.2g; Carbohydrate 3.1g, of which sugars 3.1g; Fat 6.7g, of which saturates 4.2g; Cholesterol 17mg; Calcium 7mg; Fibre 0g; Sodium 3mg.

Glasgow punch

Over the last few centuries, the Glaswegians enjoyed the rum that came over from the Caribbean with the sugar shipments. A number of drinks and cocktails were invented using rum as the base, the Glasgow punch being a favourite.

Makes 1.5 litres/3 pints

900ml/1½ pints/3¾ cups water

200g/6oz/scant 1 cup dark brown muscovado (molasses) sugar

1 orange

1 lemon

300ml/½ pint/1¼ cups rum

1 Put the water into a pan over a medium heat. Add the sugar and stir in thoroughly, then allow the water to come to a boil. Boil rapidly to reduce the quantity by about half. Set aside to cool competely.

2 Remove the rinds from the orange and lemon with a zester or a fine grater, avoiding the pith.

3 Pour the rum into a mixing bowl and add the rinds of the lemon and orange, reserving the fruit. Cover and leave to infuse overnight.

4 Squeeze the juice from the orange and lemon, then strain. Add to the bowl with the rum. Stir to mix, then strain the mixture to remove the rind.

5 Add the boiled water and sugar to taste and then bottle the punch. Drink the punch hot.

Per batch Energy 1474kcal/6206kJ; Protein 1.4g; Carbohydrate 214g, of which sugars 214g; Fat 0.1g, of which saturates 0g; Cholesterol 0mg; Calcium 113mg; Fibre 0.1g; Sodium 17mg.

Atholl brose

This is the perfect celebratory drink, with plenty of alcohol and enough "sustenance" to keep you going through a long night of drinking and dancing.

Serves 4

200g/7oz/2 cups medium rolled oats

150ml/¼ pint/⅔ cup water

115g/4oz/½ cup heather honey

900ml/1½ pints/3¾ cups Highland or Island whisky

1 Place the rolled oats in a small bowl with the water and leave for 1 hour, then stir to make a paste.

2 Press the rolled oats complete with the soaking water through a sieve into a large mixing bowl. Add the heather honey and mix thoroughly until completely combined.

3 Pour in the whisky a little at a time, stirring it in completely before adding more. Finally, stir well then pour into small whisky glasses. Keep the drink in bottles and shake well before use.

Per batch Energy 3006kcal/12559kJ; Protein 25.2g; Carbohydrate 229.6g, of which sugars 84g; Fat 17.4g, of which saturates 0g; Cholesterol 0mg; Calcium 116mg; Fibre 13.6g; Sodium 78mg.

Brammle kir

This delicious Scottish version of French Kir and Kir Royale uses either white or sparkling wine mixed with Brammle, a whisky liqueur made with blackberries. Serve as an aperitif.

Serves 1

30ml/2 tbsp Brammle liqueur

dry white wine, such as Chardonnay or Sauvignon Blanc, chilled

Variation
For a special occasion, make a Brammle Royale by replacing the white wine with chilled Champagne or fizzy wine.

1 Pour the liqueur into the bottom of a large wine glass.

2 Top up to within 2cm/¾in of the top with the chilled white wine. Enjoy!

Per portion Energy 244kcal/1017kJ; Protein 0.3g; Carbohydrate 11.3g, of which sugars 11.3g; Fat 0g, of which saturates 0g; Cholesterol 0mg; Calcium 24mg; Fibre 0g; Sodium 14mg.

Breads, bakes and preserves

The tradition of making cakes, bakes and
preserves has been part of the Scottish heritage
for hundreds of years, partly as a result of the
French influences from the Auld Alliance, and
partly due to the large quantities of sugar
imported into Glasgow from the Caribbean.
Jams and chutneys were mastered so that the
wonderful flavour and nutrients of summer
fruits could be captured and enjoyed during
the long winter months.

Traditional bannock

This is an all-purpose bread that makes an excellent breakfast with butter and jams, a teatime staple toasted with butter and honey, or an accompaniment for dunking into soups and stews.

Makes 2 loaves

175g/6oz/generous ¾ cup soft light brown sugar

450ml/¾ pint/scant 2 cups milk

25g/1oz fresh yeast or 10ml/ 2 tsp dried

1kg/2¼lb/9 cups strong white bread flour

pinch of salt

115g/4oz/½ cup butter

115g/4oz/½ cup lard or white cooking fat

450g/1lb/generous 3 cups raisins

1 Preheat the oven to 220°C/425°F/ Gas 7. Dissolve 10ml/2 tsp of the sugar in a little of the milk for the glaze.

2 Warm a little milk, add the yeast with 5ml/1 tsp of sugar, mix to dissolve the sugar and yeast then leave to activate.

3 Put the flour with the salt in a warm place. Melt the butter and lard or white cooking fat with the remaining milk and keep warm. Mix the yeast mixture with the flour then add the milk and fat mixture. Mix together until a stiff dough forms. Knead for a few minutes, cover with a clean dish towel and leave in a warm place until it doubles in size.

4 Knock back (punch down) the dough then knead in the raisins and the remaining sugar. Shape into two rounds. Place on an oiled baking sheet, cover with a clean dish towel and leave to rise again in a warm place, until about twice the size.

5 Bake in the preheated oven for 10 minutes, then reduce the heat to 190°C/375°F/Gas 5 for about 30 minutes. Fifteen minutes before they are cooked, glaze the bannocks with the reserved milk and sugar mixture.

Per portion Energy 1924kcal/8114kJ; Protein 30.6g; Carbohydrate 330.5g, of which sugars 140g; Fat 62.5g, of which saturates 30.7g; Cholesterol 103mg; Calcium 584mg; Fibre 10g; Sodium 322mg.

Drop scones

Variously known as girdlecakes, griddlecakes and Scotch pancakes, these make a quick and easy breakfast, elevensies or teatime snacks served with butter and drizzled with honey.

Makes 8–10

115g/4oz/1 cup plain (all-purpose) flour

5ml/1 tsp bicarbonate of soda (baking soda)

5ml/1 tsp cream of tartar

25g/1oz/2 tbsp butter, diced

1 egg, beaten

about 150ml/¼ pint/⅔ cup milk

a knob (pat) of butter and heather honey, to serve

1 Lightly grease a griddle pan or heavy frying pan, then preheat it. Sift the flour, bicarbonate of soda and cream of tartar together into a mixing bowl. Add the diced butter and rub it into the flour with your fingertips until the mixture resembles fine, evenly textured breadcrumbs.

2 Make a well in the centre of the flour mixture, then stir in the egg. Add the milk a little at a time, stirring it in to check consistency. Add enough milk to give a lovely thick creamy consistency.

Cook's Tip
Placing the cooked scones in a clean folded dish towel keeps them soft and moist. Bring to the table like this and ask your guests to pull them out.

3 Cook in batches. Drop 3 or 4 evenly sized spoonfuls of the mixture, spaced slightly apart, on the griddle or frying pan. Cook over a medium heat for 2–3 minutes, until bubbles rise to the surface and burst.

4 Turn the scones over and cook for a further 2–3 minutes, until golden underneath. Place the cooked scones between the folds of a clean dish towel while cooking the remaining batter. Serve warm, with butter and honey.

Per portion Energy 90kcal/379kJ; Protein 2.8g; Carbohydrate 12.1g, of which sugars 1.1g; Fat 3.8g, of which saturates 2.1g; Cholesterol 32mg; Calcium 47mg; Fibre 0.5g; Sodium 36mg.

Scottish morning rolls

These superb rolls are best served warm, as soon as they are baked. In Scotland they are a firm favourite for breakfast, served with a fried egg and bacon. They also go very well with a pat of fresh butter and homemade jams and jellies.

Makes 10

450g/1lb/4 cups unbleached plain (all-purpose) white flour, plus extra for dusting

10ml/2 tsp salt

20g/¾oz fresh yeast

150ml/¼ pint/⅔ cup lukewarm milk, plus extra for glazing

150ml/¼ pint/⅔ cup lukewarm water

1 Grease two baking sheets. Sift the flour and salt together into a large bowl and make a well in the centre. Mix the yeast with the milk, then mix in the water. Stir to dissolve. Add the yeast mixture to the centre of the flour and mix together to form a soft dough.

2 Knead the dough lightly then cover with lightly oiled clear film (plastic wrap) and leave to rise in a warm place for 1 hour, or until doubled in size. Turn the dough out on to a floured surface and knock back (punch down).

3 Divide the dough into 10 equal pieces. Knead each roll lightly and, using a rolling pin, shape each piece to a flat 10 x 7.5cm/4 x 3in oval or a flat 9cm/3½in round.

4 Transfer the rolls to the prepared baking sheets and cover with oiled clear film. Leave to rise in a warm place for about 30 minutes. Meanwhile, preheat the oven to 200°C/400°F/Gas 6.

5 Remove the clear film – the rolls should have risen slightly. Press each roll in the centre with your three middle fingers to equalize the air bubbles and to help prevent blistering.

6 Brush with milk and dust with flour. Bake for 15–20 minutes, or until lightly browned. As soon as you have taken the rolls out of the oven, dust with more flour and cool slightly on a wire rack. Serve warm.

Per roll Energy 160kcal/682kJ; Protein 4.7g; Carbohydrate 35.7g, of which sugars 1.4g; Fat 0.8g, of which saturates 0.3g; Cholesterol 1mg; Calcium 81mg; Fibre 1.4g; Sodium 401mg.

Oatmeal biscuits

Although not as neat as bought ones, these home-made oatmeal crackers make up in flavour and interest anything they might lose in presentation – and they make the ideal partner for most Scottish cheeses with some fresh fruit to accompany.

Makes about 18

75g/3oz/⅔ cup plain (all-purpose) flour

2.5ml/½ tsp salt

1.5ml/¼ tsp baking powder

115g/4oz/1 cup fine pinhead oatmeal, plus extra for sprinkling

65g/2½oz/generous ¼ cup white vegetable fat (shortening)

1 Preheat the oven to 200°C/400°F/ Gas 6 and grease a baking sheet.

2 Sift the flour, salt and baking powder into a mixing bowl. Add the oatmeal and mix well. Rub in the fat to make a crumbly mixture.

3 Blend in enough water to work the mixture into a stiff dough.

Cook's Tip
Store the biscuits when absolutely cold in an airtight container lined with baking parchment. Check for crispness before serving; reheat for 4–5 minutes in a preheated oven at 200°C/400°F/ Gas 6 to crisp up if necessary.

4 Turn on to a worktop sprinkled with fine oatmeal and knead until smooth and manageable. Roll out to about 3mm/⅛in thick and cut into rounds, squares or triangles. Place on the baking sheet.

5 Bake in the preheated oven for about 15 minutes, until crisp. Cool the biscuits on a wire rack.

Per biscuit Energy 72kcal/301kJ; Protein 1.2g; Carbohydrate 7.9g, of which sugars 0.1g; Fat 4.2g, of which saturates 1.8g; Cholesterol 3mg; Calcium 9mg; Fibre 0.6g; Sodium 57mg.

Tea loaf

It is always good to have a cake in the home, and fruit cakes are something of a tradition in Scotland. This is a simple fruit cake made by soaking dried fruits in cold tea.

Makes 1 cake

450g/1lb/2⅔ cups mixed dried fruit

250g/9oz/generous 1 cup soft light brown sugar

200ml/7fl oz/scant 1 cup cold tea

400g/1lb/4 cups self-raising (self-rising) flour

5ml/1 tsp mixed (apple pie) spice

1 egg, beaten

1 Mix the dried fruit and sugar together, pour the cold tea over and leave to soak overnight.

2 The next day, preheat the oven to 190°C/375°F/Gas 5. Line a loaf tin (pan) with baking parchment. Add the flour and spice to the soaked fruit, stirring to combine well, then add the beaten egg and mix thoroughly.

3 Put the cake mixture in the prepared loaf tin and bake in the preheated oven for 45–50 minutes. Test with a skewer, which should come out clean. If there is any cake mixture sticking to the skewer, return the cake to the oven for a few more minutes.

Variation
For something a little more special, add 10ml/2 tsp whisky to the tea to give the loaf an aromatic and sumptuous flavour. Add more if you want a really strong flavour – some people replace the tea entirely with whisky blended with a little water.

Per portion Energy 1012kcal/4316kJ; Protein 15.9g; Carbohydrate 245g, of which sugars 152.1g; Fat 3.4g, of which saturates 0.6g; Cholesterol 48mg; Calcium 569mg; Fibre 6.6g; Sodium 531mg.

Glamis walnut and date cake

This is a wonderfully rich and moist cake perfect for afternoon tea. The dates are first soaked before being added to the cake mixture. This gives the cake a lovely texture.

Makes 1 cake

225g/8oz/1⅓ cups chopped dates

250ml/8fl oz/1 cup boiling water

5ml/1 tsp bicarbonate of soda (baking soda)

225g/8oz/generous 1 cup caster (superfine) sugar

1 egg, beaten

275g/10oz/2¼ cups plain (all-purpose) flour

2.5ml/½ tsp salt

75g/3oz/6 tbsp butter, softened

5ml/1 tsp vanilla extract

5ml/1 tsp baking powder

50g/2oz/½ cup chopped walnuts

1 Put the chopped dates into a warm, dry bowl and pour the boiling water over the top; it should just cover the dates. Add the bicarbonate of soda and mix in thoroughly. Leave to stand for 5–10 minutes.

2 Preheat the oven to 180°C/350°F/ Gas 4. Lightly grease a 23 x 30cm/ 9 x 12in cake tin (pan) and line with baking parchment.

3 In a separate mixing bowl, combine all the remaining ingredients for the cake. Then mix in the dates, along with the soaking water until you have a thick batter. You may find it necessary to add a little more boiling water to help the consistency.

4 Pour or spoon the batter into the tin and bake in the oven for 45 minutes. Cut into thick wedges when cool.

Per portion Energy 749kcal/3155kJ; Protein 10.5g; Carbohydrate 125.5g, of which sugars 77.8g; Fat 26.2g, of which saturates 11g; Cholesterol 88mg; Calcium 153mg; Fibre 3.4g; Sodium 141mg.

Bramble jam

Blackberrying is a pleasant recreation and leads to a range of culinary delights too, including this jam. Serve with hot buttered toast, or scones hot from the oven and a dollop of thick clotted cream for a marvellous afternoon treat.

Makes 3.6kg/8lb

2.75kg/6lb/13¾ cups granulated white sugar

2.75kg/6lb/16 cups blackberries

juice of 2 lemons

150ml/¼ pint/⅔ cup water

Cook's Tip
The heating of the sugar in advance helps speed up the actual jam-making process and gives a brighter, more intense flavour.

1 Put the sugar to warm either in a low oven or in a pan over a low heat.

2 Wash the blackberries and place in a large pan with the lemon juice and water. Bring to the boil and simmer for about 5 minutes.

3 Stir in the sugar and bring back to the boil then boil rapidly. You will know when setting point is achieved as a spoonful of jam put on a plate and allowed to cool slightly will wrinkle when pressed. Ladle into warmed sterilized jam jars and seal immediately.

Per batch Energy 12570kcal/53550kJ; Protein 42g; Carbohydrate 3288g, of which sugars 3288g; Fat 6g, of which saturates 0g; Cholesterol 0mg; Calcium 2820mg; Fibre 93g; Sodium 240mg.

Damson jam

Dark, plump damsons used to be found growing only in the wild, but today they are available commercially. They produce a deeply coloured and richly flavoured jam that makes a tasty snack spread on toasted Scotch pancakes or warm crumpets at teatime.

Makes about 2kg/4½lb

1kg/2¼lb damsons or wild plums

1.4 litres/2¼ pints/6 cups water

1kg/2¼lb/5 cups preserving or granulated white sugar, warmed

Cook's Tip
It is important to seal the jars as soon as you have filled them to ensure the jam remains sterile. However, you should then leave the jars to cool completely before labelling and storing them, to avoid the risk of burns.

1 Put the damsons in a preserving pan and pour in the water. Bring to the boil then reduce the heat and simmer gently until the damsons are soft. Add the sugar and stir it in thoroughly. Bring the mixture to the boil.

2 Skim off the stones (pits) as they rise to the surface. Boil to setting point (105°C/220°F). Remove from the heat, leave to cool for 10 minutes, then transfer to warmed sterilized jam jars. Seal immediately.

Per batch Energy 4300kcal/18360kJ; Protein 11g; Carbohydrate 1133g, of which sugars 1133g; Fat 1g, of which saturates 0g; Cholesterol 0mg; Calcium 660mg; Fibre 16g; Sodium 80mg.

Cranberry and red onion relish

This wine-enriched relish is perfect for serving with hot roast game at a celebratory meal. It is also good served with cold meats or stirred into a beef or game casserole for a touch of sweetness. It can be made several months in advance of any festive season.

Makes about 900g/2lb

450g/1lb small red onions

30ml/2 tbsp olive oil

225g/8oz/generous 1 cup soft light brown sugar

450g/1lb/4 cups cranberries

120ml/4fl oz/½ cup red wine vinegar

120ml/4fl oz/½ cup red wine

15ml/1 tbsp yellow mustard seeds

2.5ml/½ tsp ground ginger

30ml/2 tbsp orange liqueur or port

salt and ground black pepper

1 Halve the red onions and slice them very thinly. Heat the oil in a large pan, add the onions and cook over a very low heat for about 15 minutes, stirring occasionally, until softened. Add 30ml/ 2 tbsp of the sugar and cook for a further 5 minutes, or until the onions are brown and caramelized.

2 Meanwhile, put the cranberries in a pan with the remaining sugar, and add the vinegar, red wine, mustard seeds and ginger. Stir in thoroughly and heat gently, stirring continuously, until the sugar has dissolved, then cover and bring to the boil.

3 Simmer the relish for 12–15 minutes then add the caramelized onions. Stir them into the mixture. Increase the heat slightly and cook uncovered for a further 10 minutes, stirring the mixture frequently, until well reduced and nicely thickened.

4 Remove the pan from the heat then season to taste with salt and ground black pepper. Allow to cool completely in the pan before pouring.

5 Transfer the relish to warmed sterilized jars. Spoon a little of the orange liqueur or port over the top of each, then cover and seal. This relish can be stored for up to 6 months. Store in the refrigerator once opened and use within 1 month.

Variation
Redcurrants make a very good substitute for cranberries in this recipe. They produce a relish with a lovely flavour and pretty colour.

Per batch Energy 1532kcal/6486kJ; Protein 8g; Carbohydrate 314.6g, of which sugars 304.2g; Fat 23.3g, of which saturates 3.1g; Cholesterol 0mg; Calcium 259mg; Fibre 13.5g; Sodium 46mg.

Chunky pear and walnut chutney

This chutney recipe is ideal for using up hard windfall pears. Its mellow flavour is well suited to being brought out with a lovely selection of strong Scottish cheeses served with freshly made oatcakes or a warm traditional bannock.

Makes about 1.8kg/4lb

1.2kg/2½lb firm pears

225g/8oz cooking apples

225g/8oz onions

450ml/¾ pint/scant 2 cups cider vinegar

175g/6oz/generous 1 cup sultanas (golden raisins)

finely grated rind and juice of 1 orange

400g/14oz/2 cups granulated white sugar

115g/4oz/1 cup walnuts, roughly chopped

2.5ml/½ tsp ground cinnamon

1 Peel and core the fruit, then chop into 2.5cm/1in chunks. Peel and quarter the onions, then chop into pieces the same size as the fruit chunks. Place in a large preserving pan with the vinegar.

2 Slowly bring to the boil, then reduce the heat and simmer for 40 minutes, until the apples, pears and onions are tender, stirring the mixture occasionally.

3 Meanwhile, put the sultanas in a small bowl, pour over the orange juice and leave to soak.

4 Add the orange rind, sultanas and orange juice, and the sugar to the pan. Heat gently, stirring continuously, until the sugar has completely dissolved, then leave to simmer for 30–40 minutes, or until the chutney is thick and no excess liquid remains. Stir frequently towards the end of cooking to prevent the chutney from sticking to the base of the pan.

5 Gently toast the walnuts in a non-stick pan over a low heat for 5 minutes, stirring frequently, until lightly coloured. Stir the nuts into the chutney with the ground cinnamon.

6 Spoon the chutney into warmed sterilized jars, cover and seal. Store in a cool, dark place and leave to mature for at least 1 month. Use within 1 year.

Per batch Energy 3506kcal/14818kJ; Protein 30.9g; Carbohydrate 705.4g, of which sugars 699.5g; Fat 81.4g, of which saturates 6.4g; Cholesterol 0mg; Calcium 634mg; Fibre 40.7g; Sodium 118mg.

Index